CROSS-CULTURAL ESSENTIALS 9

CHURCH PLANTING CASE STUDIES

EXAMPLES FROM AROUND THE WORLD
OF CROSS-CULTURAL CHURCH PLANTING

Church Planting Case Studies
Examples from around the world of cross-cultural church planting

Church Foundations, Module 9 of the Cross-Cultural Essentials Curriculum

Copyright © 2019 AccessTruth

Version 1.0

ISBN: 978-0-6484151-6-9

All Rights Reserved. Except as may be permitted by the Copyright Act, no part of this publication may be reproduced in any form or by any means without prior permission from the publisher. Requests for permission should be made to info@accesstruth.com

Unless otherwise indicated, all Scripture quotations are taken from the Holy Bible, New Living Translation, copyright © 1996, 2004. Used by permission of Tyndale House Publishers, Inc., Wheaton, Illinois 60189. All rights reserved.

Published by AccessTruth
PO Box 8087
Baulkham Hills NSW 2153
Australia

Email: info@accesstruth.com
Web: accesstruth.com

Cover Design by Matthew Hillier
Edited by Simon Glover

Table of Contents

About the Cross-Cultural Essentials Curriculum 5

TUTORIAL 9.1 7
Introduction

TUTORIAL 9.2 15
Snapshot of the contexts

TUTORIAL 9.3 33
Access to the Bible

TUTORIAL 9.4 41
Engaging at a worldview level

TUTORIAL 9.5 51
The authority of God's word

TUTORIAL 9.6 61
The complete Narrative

TUTORIAL 9.7 67
Making use of God's Word

TUTORIAL 9.8 73
Understanding true identity

TUTORIAL 9.9 85
The narrative of the Church

TUTORIAL 9.10 93
One body in Christ

TUTORIAL 9.11 99
Viewing others according to truth

TUTORIAL 9.12 107
God's representatives

TUTORIAL 9.13 113
A relationship with Jesus

TUTORIAL 9.14 125
The purpose for which we exist

TUTORIAL 9.15 133
Understanding God's purposes

TUTORIAL 9.16 139
Form, function, fulfilment

TUTORIAL 9.17 149
Reproducing this life

TUTORIAL 9.18 155
Disciples of the Master

TUTORIAL 9.19 161
Real-life applications

TUTORIAL 9.20 167
Applying Truth in the walk of faith

TUTORIAL 9.21 173
Equipped for service 1

TUTORIAL 9.22 181
Equipped for service 2

About the Cross-Cultural Essentials Curriculum

It's no secret that there are still millions of people in the world living in "unreached" or "least-reached" areas. If you look at the maps, the stats, and the lists of people group names, it's almost overwhelming. The people represented by those numbers can't find out about God, or who Jesus Christ is, or what He did for them because there's no Bible in their language or church in their area – they have *no access* to Truth.

So you could pack a suitcase and jump on a plane, but then what? How would you spend your first day? How would you start learning language? When would you tell them about Jesus? Where would you start? The truth is that a mature, grounded fellowship of God's children doesn't just "happen" in an unreached area or even in your neighbourhood. When we speak the Truth, we need to have the confidence that it is still the same Truth when it gets through our hearer's language, culture and worldview grid.

The *Cross-Cultural Essentials* curriculum, made up of 10 individual modules, forms a comprehensive training course. Its main goal is to help equip believers to be effective in providing people access to God's Truth through evangelism and discipleship. The *Cross-Cultural Essentials* curriculum makes it easy to be better equipped for teaching the whole narrative of the Bible, for learning about culture and worldview and for planting a church and seeing it grow.

More information on the curriculum can be found at *accesstruth.com*

Introduction to Module 9

The Church Planting Case Studies in this course, (Module 9 of the AccessTruth curriculum) are framed by the categories Word, Identity, Life, Discipleship. When this framework was introduced in Module 7, it was not with a specific context in view. The four W.I.L.D areas were discussed in turn, with the intention of demonstrating how the principles relate to any situation in which God's Word is being shared and discipleship is taking place.

This Module also makes applications from those W.I.L.D. areas, but in the form of case studies, all of which relate to work done in people groups where God's Word was previously absent or difficult to access; in other words, cross-cultural, church planting and discipleship scenarios. The 22 tutorials contain a wealth of valuable insights from church planters and first generation church leaders as they reflect on the challenges they've faced, and also the amazing fruit they've seen in the areas of God's Word, Identity, Life and Discipleship.

These tutorials are transcripts of the videos found at accesstruth.com

ABOUT THE CROSS-CULTURAL ESSENTIALS CURRICULUM

How to use this module

Read / watch / listen: Read through the tutorial. If you have an online account at *accesstruth.com*, or the DVD associated with this module you can watch the video or listen to the audio of the tutorial.

Discussion Points: At the end of each tutorial there are discussion points. It may be helpful to write down your answers so you can better process your thoughts. If you are doing the tutorials in a group, use these points to guide the discussion.

Activities: Some tutorials have activities that can involve practical, real-life tasks or may just ask for a written answer.

9.1 Introduction

✓ OBJECTIVES OF THIS TUTORIAL

This tutorial introduces Module 9 and its presenters. It also recaps the key concepts of the W.I.L.D. framework.

Welcome to Module 9 of the AccessTruth Curriculum. Throughout this module you will be introduced to a number of people working in different parts of the globe. You will hear some of their stories in a range of church planting contexts from around the world. We've put their descriptions into a framework of Word, Identity, Life, and Discipleship, the WILD framework.

But before getting into that, we'd like to introduce Rich Brown. Rich and his wife Karen worked for many years in a previously unreached people group in Indonesia. We invited Rich to have a part in Module 9 based on his experience in church planting:

> It's a pleasure to be here. Yeah, we, my family and myself, served among people called the Moi. We lived there in Asia Pacific with them for a good number of years. Before the team moved in to live with them in early 2000, the Moi were pretty much unknown to the world. And they didn't have any Gospel witness. They had never heard of Christ, basically they'd been living the way they have for years, centuries. It was the Lord who brought a team together to share His Word with them because He loved them, even though they didn't yet know Him.
>
> Learning their language and culture took a few years, and eventually we reached the place where we could begin to communicate God's Word to them. And as His Word says it doesn't return void. And we saw that play out in their lives. We had opportunity to see it communicated to them in a way they could understand. We taught them foundationally starting in Genesis and gave them a good concept of who God is. We had to actually come up with a name for the Creator, taking the verb "to create" and making it into a noun.

INTRODUCTION

God is the Creator so we talked about the Creator and His great love for them through creation, and how He loved mankind and created this planet for us. And then we introduced the fall, of course, and they identified themselves with Adam in the fall and their need to have a relationship with Him, and they wanted that.

So we saw just a small group initially respond, only eight actually, but we knew that it was just the beginning. And over the years, the Lord provided more opportunities to teach His Word, and more people who have come to know Him, and the church has really grown. And today we have people who are carrying on a lot of the same responsibility that we had. He's allowed us to see disciples made, not of us but of Christ. They love the Lord deeply and are willing to lay their lives down for one another.

It's amazing when you think about it. They were people who were actually incredibly selfish and self-centered, like we all are. Then the Holy Spirit entered into them and now they're walking with the Lord, they are quite selfless, and we've seen them be radically changed. And today they're serving one another and they're reaching out to people who haven't yet heard within their own tribe and now actually in other places as well. So yeah, it's pretty, pretty amazing.

So now we have elders in the church, and they're leading the church, and our coworkers, Steven and Carolyn, are still there finishing up the Bible translation. And we hope to see that done shortly. And myself, we've been able to now move on, and take on more responsibility to help others who are endeavoring to do the same things and I'm a mentor to people groups outside of the Moi area. I'm now helping as a consultant and providing help to others who are looking to the Lord to do the same type of things, working and reaching the unreached people groups.

We've had experience in seeing the Lord do some pretty cool things among the Moi, and we learned a whole lot along the way. I think if we were to do it over again, we would do some things differently for sure. But yeah, it's now an opportunity for us to be able to help others, and maybe they might not make some of the same mistakes. And it's been really neat to be able to visit some of the other ministry contexts, and to be able to speak into some of those things at times, and learn a lot, actually, along the way seeing as these contexts are not all the same. The challenges are not all the same. But a lot of times the principles that we are learning along the way can apply to these different locations and be of help. That's really our hearts' desire as we, my family and myself, are involved in trying to help others do well in the work the Lord has called them to.

We'd also like to introduce Paul McIlwain. Paul and his wife Linda worked for eleven years in Papua New Guinea doing pioneering church planting work and Bible translation among a previously unreached people group. They have since been involved in church planting consultancy giving guidance to teams all around the world. They are passionate about seeing churches planted that are well equipped to carry on for future generations:

> We, my wife and I, worked in Papua New Guinea. We went there in the late '80's and we had the opportunity to go into a situation not all that dissimilar from Rich Brown's. I know that the area he was in was very remote and very, very cut off from the outside world. The situation we went into was a mountainous area that was cut off but not quite to the same degree, so that the people we worked with, that we lived among and got to know and really came to appreciate, had had some exposure to, let's say, a form of Christianity and to a church of some kind. But that had been heavily syncretized with their traditional animistic beliefs. And a local cult had existed in that area, a prosperity cult.
>
> So there was a very confused worldview picture there. Their story, their narrative, was a very confused one with a lot of different influences coming in. So we had the opportunity to go in there and, like Rich Brown and his family, to learn their language and understand their culture to a degree, I guess as much as we were able. We lived in a small community up in the mountains and eventually shared God's Word, His Narrative and we saw a response, a tremendous response.
>
> You feel the privilege of that, of being observers of things that God is doing. And yes, there's hard work involved and application and commitment, but really more and more you have this sense that you're observing, watching the things that God's doing through His Word. And I hope and trust that something that's going to come out through this material, through these resources, is a strong sense of dependence on God.
>
> So we had the opportunity to be involved in a translation project and to see a literacy program developed and eventually to see a number of churches established in that area and then reach out, even cross culturally. Today there are a number of churches existing there. And we continue to go back and visit, but it's been some time.

INTRODUCTION

W.I.L.D.

Now we're going to look at the content of this module to give you an idea of what we're covering. You may have already seen Module 7 of the AccessTruth Curriculum. This module is in some ways based on Module 7 in which we introduce WILD and what we call the WILD framework. It's a way of looking at any context in which truth is being shared through the lenses of Word, Identity, Life, and Discipleship.

For the purpose of this module, we're focusing on cross-cultural, pioneering church planting settings. In Module 7 we presented the material in a way that shows how these principles relate to any setting, whether that be in a western church setting or elsewhere. Wherever it is, the same principles are relevant because they come out of God's Word.

You can find the framework on the Access Truth website in the electronic version of the WILD outline. We recommend that you download it for reference as you go through this module.

Let's look at what is contained in the framework, starting with the area of Word. Each area includes questions that we can ask about any setting where truth is being shared, but again, in this context we are focusing specifically on crosscultural church planting settings.

WORD

- Are they able to access the Bible in a form that clearly and faithfully communicates God's revelation to them?
- Are they having God's Word presented to them in a way that allows it to enter and engage their hearts at a worldview level?
- Are they learning to give God's Word its proper place and authority?
- Are they growing in their ability to correctly understand God's Word as His complete Narrative, with Jesus Christ as the heart of the story and its interpretive key?
- Are they increasingly able to make use of God's Word as He intends for His children and His Church?

IDENTITY

- Are they increasingly clear about—and able to articulate —their true identity from God's perspective?
- Are they learning to see their story embedded in the larger Narrative of the Church, stretching back to Pentecost and forward to Christ's return?
- Are they growing in their understanding of the bonds that unite them to the global/local Body under Christ as its Head?
- Are they learning to view others according to truth, and rejecting the divisions, biases and tensions that often define the wider society?
- Are they growing in their understanding of how to appropriately represent the Lord in their current spheres of contact and in others He might lead them to be involved in?

LIFE

- Are they experiencing a deepening relationship with Jesus, learning to depend more completely on Him in different areas of their lives, and gradually seeing their values and behavior change as a result?
- Are they gaining clarity about the true purpose for which they exist, and are they increasingly able to identify those things that hinder their life in Christ?
- Are they increasingly able to make good decisions based on their understanding of God's local and global purposes, and to use their time, money and other resources accordingly?
- Are they learning to shape the form of what they do to serve whatever function they are convinced will lead to the fulfillment of God's objectives?
- Are they growing in their commitment to reproducing the life they have in Christ, are they equipped with the resources and skills to do so, and are they prioritizing opportunities where there is real need and hunger?

DISCIPLESHIP

- Are they seeing all other ties, loyalties and commitments being increasingly defined by their primary relationship: disciples of their Master, Jesus Christ.

- Are they being helped to apply the general truth from God's Word to their own specific real-life situations?

- Are they able to access regular, godly input and genuine friendships that intentionally help them along as they follow Jesus in the walk of faith?

- Are they being encouraged to function in the areas in which God has gifted and given them abilities so they can develop in their service to Him and His Body?

- Are they being given access to Bible-based resources that adequately equip them to be involved in the function and outreach of the Body, in local and global contexts?

Building, Body, Bride

In future tutorials we will get into some of the questions above in detail. We'll be hearing from people who talk about complex challenges surrounding these questions and their experience of seeing those challenges play out.

To conclude this particular tutorial, let's think about three primary images for the church that we find in God's Word. As we see God using these images, we are better able to picture the church from God's perspective, and to relate to it as His servants. To help us think this through, let's look at Ephesians 2:20-22:

> Together, we are his house, built on the foundation of the apostles and the prophets. And the cornerstone is Christ Jesus himself. We are carefully joined together in him, becoming a holy temple for the Lord. Through him you Gentiles are also being made part of this dwelling where God lives by his Spirit.

We are participants in what God wants to do in reaching this world and making disciples of Christ but we need to remember that we're also disciples of Christ ourselves. We're not only part of this building; we're also involved in making other parts of the same building. It's a unique picture. One of the things we see in God's Word is this great care that God has taken with the process of building His temple. This comes out in 1 Corinthians 3:10:

> Because of God's grace to me, I have laid the foundation like an expert builder. Now others are building on it. But whoever is building on this foundation must be very careful.

That's actually quite an important warning for us. You see the care that God has taken. He's very intentional about how to go about building His church, and He's giving us the privilege to be involved with that. He has planned out how it should be done and He has given us His Word as a guide. So we need to follow that blueprint and not just go about doing things our own way.

We have to take real care to ensure we are engaged on all levels, including our minds. This is important because God is not this detached architect doing this project; He's fully engaged, He's fully committed. We should be too. There's this sense of authority and connection that He has with His church, which comes out in Ephesians 4: 16- 17:

> He makes the whole body fit together perfectly. As each part does its own special work, it helps the other parts grow, so that the whole body is healthy and growing and full of love.

The apostle Paul is trying to use these different analogies to help us understand that the church is something that God loves dearly. He wants us to be able to grasp that and so he's using these different pictures. Here he uses the analogy of the body. Each believer is a member of the body—you and I and the rest of the church. We get to participate in seeing this body develop and grow and come to maturity.

There's a sense of partnership that's in this great project that God's involved in. We see a reflection of His authority, and we get to be involved by choice, by commitment. But it's not just detached or theoretical. Christ is emotionally invested in the formation of His church. Ephesians 5:25-26 reflects this picture:

> For husbands, this means love your wives, just as Christ loved the church. He gave up his life for her to make her holy and clean, washed by the cleansing of God's Word.

And then in Revelation 19:7, as we look to the fulfillment of all that God is working toward, it shows us a great vision:

> Let us be glad and rejoice, and let us give honor to him. For the time has come for the wedding feast of the Lamb, and his bride has prepared herself.

Our emotions are involved too, aren't they? We've got our intellect and our wills, our commitment and also the love that He gives us for His body, His church. We'll see that reflected in future tutorials as we look at case studies of people who are giving their lives to be involved in the task which Christ Himself, our Master, left to His church, that He loves so much and in which He has invested so much.

INTRODUCTION

❓ DISCUSSION POINTS

1. As you read about the two contexts described in this tutorial, use the following headings to note anything that you think could have been significant barriers to the Gospel.
- Physical
- Linguistic
- Cultural
- Relational
- Other challenges related to the country or context

➡ ACTIVITIES

1. Research and in a short paragraph describe 'Animism'. Note down your sources of information. (You will find a 2-part video series about Animism in AccessTruth.com)

2. Research and in a short paragraph describe 'Syncretism'. Note down your sources of information.

3. Download and read through the WILD framework e-book (found at accesstruth.com).

9.2 Snapshot of the contexts

 OBJECTIVES OF THIS TUTORIAL

This tutorial introduces the different contexts which will be referred to during the interviews in this module.

Last Time

We reminded ourselves of the WILD outline which will provide the framework for the rest of this Module. We looked at the purpose of WILD and talked about how it can apply in cross-cultural church planting situations and also where a church already exists in any setting.

Snapshots

To give you some background, the WILD outline has been widely used over a number of years. This framework, or lens, for looking at maturity came out of cross-cultural, pioneering church planting situations.

It's easy in the context to start losing sight of your end goal and to be confused about where you're going. Having a tool like WILD available is helpful because you can use it as a measuring stick, "This is where we are at now and, through the process of discipleship, this is where we want to go." It has been quite useful in seeing people move towards maturity, both individually but also as a corporate body.

Oftentimes we can become consumed with the actual work we're doing and sometimes that can be disconnected from the end goal if we're not careful. Our focus can become producing material—it could even become producing a Bible translation—and we can forget that the intent of that is so there can be a mature church. So we've got to keep those things connected well. Using the WILD framework is incredibly helpful to guide us as we move along.

Throughout this tutorial we will be hearing from experienced church planters from a variety of contexts around the world. To lay a foundation for the rest of the module, in this tutorial we will be giving a 'snapshot' of each of those contexts.

Greg and Julieann

Greg and his wife Julieann lived in a city in Siberia for over ten years working with minority people from a former Soviet republic. Of particular interest for our purpose in these tutorials was their work among a deaf subculture in that region and the fruit that they saw. Greg and Julieann continue to be involved with that church but also in much wider contexts around the world. Greg shares:

> The country of Russia changed quite a bit once the Soviet Union had collapsed. That process left few jobs available. Most of the industry was pulled out of the regions and so for much of Siberia, it was abject poverty. There was a massive increase in alcoholism which had really impacted the region, so we were the first foreigners to enter that place at a very dark time. It was a time where people were wondering if there would be any food the next day, if there would be any kind of livelihood for their future. It was a very depressing time, and as far as a government, there was a lot of uncertainty about the future. What would happen? What would it look like? So there was a huge transition taking place.
>
> When you're talking about their worldview and how that impacted their livelihood, the decay of the Soviet Union caused a sense of hopelessness. The idea of morality was eliminated. The people had been raised under a Communist system which had thrived in this area. There was no God and therefore no moral value, no moral right. They were struggling with what that meant for them as people. Darkness and hopelessness were probably the most predominant feelings that existed in the area. It was visible in almost every part of their lives. The value of life was gone. You would see people who had died and were lying on the streets and not being moved or touched by anybody, just because the lack of care had gone. It was a society that was just empty.
>
> When we arrived in the place where we lived, I would say there was a rediscovery of Buddhism taking place. Christianity wasn't really predominant in the region that we were in. There was an Orthodox church that had existed under the Soviet Union that was still alive at that time, but it had very little power in the region. It had almost no understanding of what Christianity was or who God was.
>
> This sort of resurgence for Buddhism had begun among the people. Buddhist temples were being built again and there was a sort of return to Buddhism, but there was a very strong shamanistic veneer that had been placed over the whole thing.

There were two sides to the people group that we worked in. One side was more shamanistic, the other side was more Buddhist. Yet, the whole veneer of the whole country was shamanistic in a lot of ways.

We found that it was very difficult to go to our area as a missionary and so we found other ways to get into the country that built relationships. Finding ways to build relationships was fairly difficult, being from the nationality that I was from. They weren't exactly open to Americans and to the American mindset. Yet there was also this kind of sense that there must be something better out there. So building relationships took a lot of time, especially amongst men. We began by building relationships with deaf people. These were some of the poorest of the poor and some of the people who had suffered the most persecution under that regime. So they were desperate for jobs and a livelihood and we began to develop a relationship with them, partly because we were learning the language and they didn't speak the national language (verbally anyway). So we began learning their language and began building relationships with them.

Dave and Nancy

Another snapshot from a very different context and climate is Dave and his wife Nancy. They lived and worked in a difficult-to-reach people group on an island off Papua New Guinea. They had the opportunity to see the full scope of church planting work from Dave's primary role as translator. He has spent many years since as a translation consultant and cross-cultural trainer. Dave tells us:

The people live in a very remote area of New Britain Island. It's just dense jungle. There are no roads going there. Generally, they would have to hike through the jungle for one or two days to get to a major river or to the coast. It's lowland, tropical rain forest, it's hot and has a very high annual rainfall. The people there do subsistence farming. They cut down areas of the jungle and grow their food. They're really not very dependent on the outside world at all.

There was no nearby medical help available when we first went there. It was estimated that the infant mortality rate was about 55%, which means more than half of the babies didn't make it to their first birthday, and that's because it would take about two or three days to get out to the provincial capital, where the closest hospital was. They knew by past experience that if they had a very sick child and tried to make that journey, generally the baby would die en route, so they mostly just did not attempt it.

SNAPSHOT OF THE CONTEXTS

As far as education, the government established a primary school in our area, but it was very difficult to get the teachers to stay there. The teachers would come from other parts of the country and had grown accustomed to living in town and I think, pretty much without exception, the teachers that were allocated to our area viewed it as a stepping stone and a temporary allocation. They looked forward to a better allocation, from their perspective, closer to town. If there was a national holiday that was supposed to be a three-day weekend, they would go to town for that holiday and it might be a month before they came back, so the kids that attended this school did not get a very good education. There's a test that they would take at the end of year six to see if they qualified to go to high school, and pretty much none of the kids that went through that school would qualify. It's not that they weren't intelligent enough, but the teachers just weren't there consistently enough to give them a reasonable education.

Well, when the people in that area look at the world around them, they see a vast array of spiritual forces, personal spirits and also impersonal spiritual forces. They need to know how to avoid these or how to manipulate them because these forces can have a very negative effect on their lives. In fact, every major event that they see in the physical realm has some kind of spiritual cause, such as death, serious illness, a garden that produces food well or that doesn't produce food. There is some kind of identifiable spiritual cause in their mind, and to be able to survive, they need to learn how to manipulate and control these spirit beings and impersonal spiritual forces.

The people had nominally been exposed to Catholicism. There was a small Catholic church building about 30 minutes away from the village we lived in. There was never a priest located there. They had Catholic catechists who were married with children. They came from a different part of the country, and when we first started teaching them, I think we overestimated the depth to which this Catholicism had gone. We found that really it was just a very thin veneer over deep, deep animistic beliefs.

For many of them, going to that church every Sunday morning was nothing more than just a social gathering. There were three other villages and many of them would gather every Sunday morning there. They would take some of their fruits and vegetables to sell at a market and I think they would catch up on the community news. It really was more of a social gathering than a deeply religious gathering. I won't say that's true for 100% of them, some of them probably were serious about following Catholic beliefs, but for most of them it wasn't anything that went very deep at all.

They didn't have a well filled out understanding of God. They had a being that they said, in their history, created the taro, which is their main staple food. Beyond that, they didn't really know very much about him, so they didn't really have a clear picture of any kind of supreme being. It really was more just the spirit beings and spiritual forces.

We first made contact with these people in 1980 and started making trips in there to build houses. Once it was agreed that we would locate in one particular village, we started building houses. We started on an airstrip which actually took more than three years to complete, but then once our house building was basically finished, we started learning their culture and their language, and we started building relationships with them, gaining their trust, becoming their friends, so that eventually there would be a reason for them to listen to what we had to say.

John and Betty

Another snapshot is John and his wife Betty who lived on an Indonesian island with a people group who were quite cut off from the outside world. The church planting team they were part of faced significant challenges as they brought God's Word to a community that was oppressed by formidable traditional taboos. After establishing the church there, John and Betty have since been giving guidance and training to cross-cultural workers in Australia and beyond:

It was 1982 when we first moved in amongst the people of Halmahera Island on the Provence of Maluku in Indonesia. They were a completely unreached people group. They knew nothing of the Bible at that time and had no portions of the Bible in their own language. They were a very difficult group to get to and I think that may be one of the reasons why they were unreached at that point in time. In order to get there, we had to do quite a bit of boat travel, and there were moments where we almost drowned on a number of occasions—actually a boat on one occasion did sink. So it was a difficult work in that it was extremely remote.

It was also difficult because they were monolingual so we couldn't use Indonesian at all with them, which made it very challenging. The third reason that it was difficult was that they were a completely illiterate group and had no exposure to any sort of education. They were seminomadic hunters and gatherers, so we would think we had a group around us for a little while and then we could wake up the next morning and they'd all be gone somewhere else.

SNAPSHOT OF THE CONTEXTS

In the villages around the area that they roamed and out in the township that we based ourselves in, people were very nervous—nervous for us when they heard we were moving in amongst this people group. Some of the people who we developed friendships with were quite concerned for us and really thought we were crazy for going and living amongst them.

We'd heard many stories about them, like they would fly through the air and they would kill animals and tear them apart and eat the raw meat with their bare hands. So we assumed that probably some of these stories were gross exaggerations as well, but later on we found out that some of them were indeed true. In fact, there were a few attempts to dispose of us at different times, but God amazingly thwarted those attempts. As I look back now and think about the work there, I just marvel at how God looked after us that whole time, both on the sea and with the people in those early days.

They believed that if they had any contact with the church, as they perceived the church to be, someone in their family would die. They thought if a member of a family actually went to one of the village churches that were dotted along the coast and attended church, then a brother, sister, mother or father would die as a result of that. That was probably the strongest taboo and that may have also applied for Islam, although we became more aware of their beliefs to do with Christianity.

As animists they were under the domination of spirits, their lives were controlled by the spirits and they lived in fear of them. They would set pig traps that comprised of razor-sharp bamboo that was catapulted into the animal when it tripped a cord that was set in the jungle. But they believed that if they visited those traps more often than every third day, the spirit of that trap would be angry with them and that trap would never again catch any food. So you might set a trap and that night it would actually catch something, but then you couldn't retrieve it for several days. Once retrieved, they also believed that you had to consume that meat so even if it was rotten, which on occasions it was, they would still feel that they had to eat it. When we were in there, they would often come to us with stomach aches and you could actually smell them coming because of the smell from their pores and you knew that they had been eating bad meat.

They believed that twins were the result of an evil spirit, that a man could only father one child, and therefore if there was a multiple birth then that was the result of an evil spirit fathering that second child. So they would try and determine which one was the offspring of the evil spirit and that child would then be taken out and left to die. If they were unsure which child was the evil spirit, such was their degree of fear that they would take both out just to make sure that they had rid themselves of this baby that had the potential to kill them all. It was very important for the preservation of the tribe that this be done.

In talking to some of the women who had actually done that, we found that it broke their hearts to do it. Here was the baby that they had carried for nine months and now had to dispose of, and even though there was that fear, there was still some bond existing between them which made it very difficult for them to do, but they knew that they had to for the sake of the tribe.

We had a very multi-national team. There was Keith and Anita Miles and their boys from America, Don McCall from New Zealand and Heather from Australia, then Betty, me and our kids and also an Indonesian couple, Chris and Ida, who joined our team, so we had quite a mix of nationalities. Chris and Ida insisted we hold team meetings in Indonesian and I look back and think that was one of the real positives of our work. They brought an understanding of the culture and they picked up on a lot of things that we missed, and for that reason, I'm just so thankful that we had them on the team.

As the years went by, we would be out spending time with the people in their homes, trying to just absorb as much as we could of how they lived, and not only how they lived, but why they lived that way. We kept a culture file and would get together every week and compare notes of all the things that we'd discovered. We did genealogies and mapping and all the sorts of usual things that most tribal workers do.

Year started to go by and we got more and more discouraged because we thought, "Are we ever going get this language?" But the time did come when some consultants came in, and even that was a challenge because it was just so difficult to get in there, but they did come in and they checked our language and said, "Okay, a couple more months and you'll be right. Just cover a few more details and you can go ahead and start translating and preparing lessons."

So that was a wonderful time, but the thing was, we still had this taboo to deal with. Would the people actually listen to our story? I tell you what, the times when I thought to myself, "If I've spent all this time learning this rotten language and they don't listen, I am going to be very ticked off." Because, boy, that took a lot of hard work. I'm not a really gifted language learner so I had to work very hard. I think the whole team did actually.

So anyway, one day I was talking with a couple of guys and I started to tell them that we'd actually come with a message. It was great that we could help them medically and honestly, I believe the medical program was a tremendous tool for building relationships and developing that trust. That was a very tangible way of showing them that we really did care about them and building those relationships. But I said to them, "It's been great that we could do that, it's been great that we could do some things to help you economically as well, but there's another reason we came and that's the most important reason. We've come with a message, and the One who made everything that you see around you wants you to know His Story. That's why we've left our families back in Australia and America and Chris and Ida have left their families and come here to live amongst you, and we've spent all this time learning your language. It's so that we can tell you this Story."

Now by this time, they knew that we were Christians, and they were pretty wary of that, but somehow I think God had been at work building these relationships and we'd been hard at work too. So I think they were fairly confident that we were on their side, that we were there for them, we cared about them and we'd had ample opportunity to show them love. They had seen that the things that scared the daylights out of them didn't scare us, and that had a huge impact on them.

In fact, one woman said to my wife, "Why aren't you leaving the house when your neighbours die because his spirit is going to come back and get even with anyone who's offended him. We're all taking off and you need to take off too." And Betty said, "No, we're just going to stay. We're not afraid." The woman said, "Why aren't you afraid?" And Betty said, "Well, that's the real reason we've come here to live amongst you and are learning your language, so that we can tell you that." This woman said to Betty, "Oh, I hope you learn our language quickly, because we want to know that."

Phil and Elin

Phil and his wife Elin have been working in Mozambique for the last ten years in a coastal people group. Historically they have identified with Islam, and that is present to this day along with traditional animistic practices and beliefs. The team has taken a careful approach in terms of their identity to keep clear about what it is that they are bringing to the community. God is blessing them, and through the experience He is giving Phil insights that he has opportunity to share in many contexts around the world:

We came into Mozambique in January of 2004 and our intent was to work with whatever was the least reached people group in Mozambique. The first few months, we got settled in the city of Nampula and then we ended up coming and doing surveys. Our armchair research had said that this people group that we're in right now was the least reached. It had received its name from a river and we figure there's about 180,000 people who speak that language. It's a dialect of the Makua dialect which is a big, big language group in northern Mozambique.

They're one of the dialects that needed a Scripture translation in that particular dialect, according to those who investigate such things. That was the group that was on the list. It's right on the coast and so they tend to be fishermen. The main income is from fishing. It is basically the last people group, if you look at Islam coming down the East Coast of Africa, that's Islamic. After that it tapers out and becomes nominal Christian and Catholic. But in the days before, it would have just been straight out animism or paganism or whatever you'd call it. This is the last group that has a strong identity, that we are Muslim, and that makes us distinct from the people groups around us. It's one of the high identity points for them as a people group. This is what makes this group different. So coming into that then we knew ahead of time that there was going to be certain things that we were going to need to be careful about. There were going to be things that we could say that would obligate them to oppose us. The degree to which we came and associated overtly with Christianity and with the Church, to that degree you could bet money that they would be obligated to oppose whatever it was that we're doing. We'd seen and heard of examples of people coming in with a very strong Christian emphasis who had been categorically rejected by these people before, and so when we came in, you could tell that that was in their mind with the nature of the questions that they were asking. "Okay, what is this? Is this a church? How is this going to be?"

We said to them, "Hey, we're not here to build buildings, like church buildings and paint names on them. We're here to teach you what God's Word says in your language, translate it into your language, teach you how to read and write it and sit with you. We can sit under a tree and we can teach and explain everything that needs to be done under a tree. We're not here to build these buildings." In their mind, missionaries like us are coming in the name of some organisation to build that organization's kingdom in this place. We weren't wanting to perpetuate that idea. We wanted to be open and free for all the different groups to be able to come.

So when we came, we explained that to these different villages. In every location that we visited, they all said the same thing. They all said, "We'd really like for you to come and do that if you would." So we were like, "Okay, we've been invited. We've got this open door to all of these different villages. Which one are we going to choose?" So we were praying about it and we had different criteria. Some of the criteria, looking back on it, were pretty lame, but we had all these different criteria that we were thinking of, so we ended up in this particular village where the reception had been really good. They seemed really open, all the way from the top leaders down.

We were nervous about the first surveys. Are they even going to accept us and be open to us coming? We were nervous halfway through the years about whether we were going to even learn the language or not, but graciously the Lord allowed us to learn the language. We were nervous when we wanted to start teaching whether anybody would even come. We were nervous when we started teaching whether or not people were actually going to keep coming when they saw where this was going and who we were talking about. When they saw that the focus was on Jesus, would they even stick around? And if they stuck around and believed, what's going to happen in the next village when they hear that the guy we're talking about is Jesus?

We were worried that maybe we'll get these guys in this village to believe, but then what? Will that be the last village we get because it will just be shut down after that? Then we were worried are these guys going to take it and run with it and go with it, or are they going to be so secretive about it that they won't be able to speak about it publicly. So there were a lot of things that we were worried about.

As we look back on it now, we realise that the Lord was at work and all of those things took care of themselves. As they heard about His Word, they were willing to keep hearing it. When it got time to talk about Jesus, they were willing to keep sitting there, they were willing to wrestle through that and understand that it is Christ that we have to trust in and nobody else. The other villages were open to hearing and believing. We still are constantly getting requests from different villages who say, "Can you come and please teach us?" So for us it's just been amazing to see the Lord progress ahead of us and provide and work out everything that we were worried about.

Matt and Starr

Matt and his wife Starr have been working with a people group from a mountainous area in southern Mexico for over a decade. They have seen some fruit in the very difficult soil there but the recent violence related to the drug trade has had a significant impact on the work. This has created an enormously challenging church planting situation to which Matt and the team have had to respond. Matt and Starr have been involved in wider leadership, consultancy and pre-field training roles:

My name is Matt and I work with a people group in Northern Mexico. My wife Starr and I have been with them for about 20 years. We recently reengaged with the people after a short time away. We've spent the last two years getting back engaged with them and looking forward to seeing the Lord move the work forward with them in His time.

Regarding God's Word in their language, we have a co-worker who is finishing the New Testament within the next year. We're pretty excited about this people group having the New Testament. There are about 25 to 30 Christians so far. The people group numbers about 9000 and they live in the high mountains of Northern Mexico. They are drawn to folk Catholicism, a worldview system that is very animistic, very fear driven, and yet is labelled as being from the Catholic Church.

My role on the team for the last number of years has been to develop the foundational Bible teaching curriculum for them, and as such, my wife and I are some of the teachers. My wife has learned the language fluently and has many opportunities with the women to teach and disciple.

We work together as a couple. Most of our teaching opportunities are in homes with family groups of 10 to 12 adults. The people are very suspicious of outsiders and very suspicious of one another. That part of their culture has gotten worse. It's become more challenging due to the pressure from the illicit drug trade in our area and the dangers that are inherent in that situation. So that aspect of their culture, being very suspicious of outsiders, has now impacted their suspicion even of one another and so it's been very challenging to get them to come together in groups, so we've been, in a sense, forced to teach in smaller groups and to see the church gradually build in that way.

Clark and Mary

Clark and his wife Mary have worked in Thailand for many years. Along with wider leadership roles, they have been part of an effort to see a church established in a minority group in that country. Nationally Buddhist, but locally animistic, and also with an extremely low self-esteem, the community has taken a long time to embrace the Truth. But access to the Scripture, that Mary has translated and that Clark has taught, has greatly strengthened the church in recent years. Clark tells us:

We work with a people group of north-eastern Thailand. They are in north-eastern Thailand but extend across Laos and also into Vietnam. When we moved in, there was no written language. The people there have a legend that they at one time had an alphabet, but they wrote it down on a water buffalo skin and hung it out to dry and the dogs got it, so they don't have their own written language. When we first moved in, we had to develop orthography and a literacy course.

They used to live in hamlets out in the rice fields so they don't have a really strong cultural bond together. Now they would live in larger villages, anywhere from 100 to maybe 500 or 600 people per village.

> When we first moved in and we first started teaching, it was pretty much an oral presentation of the Gospel. We worked off lessons but didn't have any Scripture that we could use. If we did use Scripture, it was the Thai Scriptures. We started Bible translation about eight or nine years into the church plant. The people don't have a real desire for God's Word in their own language. They can read Thai, but we found that the more we've translated, the more they've appreciated having God's Word in their own language. We've seen that the effect of having it in their language has been more understanding and more growth.
>
> There's a group of about 100 believers, primarily the village we located in. Also, a few believers are in two or three of the other villages in that area. Totally, there're 16 villages in an area of about 40 kilometres. But right now, there are believers in three of those villages.

Bill and Kelley

Bill and Kelley are part of a church planting team in the Madang region of Papua New Guinea. The language group they work with is located in a lowlying rainforest delta. The Gospel has been welcomed now among many villages and has radically transformed their way of life. The churches are part of outreaches to neighboring people groups. Bill and Kelley are now involved in on-field equipping and leadership:

> We moved into the area in 2003 to this very, very remote location. We actually did surveys to find a place that was away from any other roads and went back to this area where there was no contact at all with the Gospel, and the people were very, very receptive of us, very animistic but very receptive of us and wanted to have us in there. The five things that we said that we were going to do was learn their language, translate the Scriptures, teach literacy, teach them the Bible, and then we were going to equip them to be able to teach others in their village.
>
> There were about 10 different villages and it was all spread out. We started right away building houses. We took chainsaws in and actually didn't take a lot of teams in with us. We used the people and tried to model that aspect of discipleship right from the very beginning of how we want to integrate them into what we're doing. It's not about what we're doing but how we're going to do this as a team. We had two girls at the time, five and seven years old, and we moved in with our team and immediately set up home school for the girls and we both worked on language. Both of us actually passed the checks that we had at the same time and were able to move right into literacy. Kelley kind of headed up the literacy programme and I started right in on Bible translation.

When we first got there, one of the things that was really interesting was that the women had just taken off, so when we first arrived in the village there were no women there. Most of the kids were gone. Some of the younger ones and older ones were there, but most of them were gone. The men had told them that we were coming in to steal their wives, so the wives gathered up everything they owned and hit the bush and hid from us initially.

Moving in, we saw a lot of rituals that they were doing. Cargo cult was a huge aspect and there were certain people in the village that were trying to promote the idea that we brought these guys in and now we're going to find out how to get all this stuff that we need.

Babies were dying like crazy because they had sorcerers that were actually doing things to cause the kids to die, so it was a really evil place. People were very friendly though. They thought that we were bringing them something. That was part of the invitation that we got to come move in with them. They thought we were going to be bringing them something and so they were very excited. They didn't know what that was, but they were very excited and they were very helpful. They gave us property and didn't charge us anything for the land. They helped us build, all with the idea that we were going to be giving them something. It was a very inviting environment for us, so the actual moving in and learning the language and asking them to help us went very smoothly in that regard.

We think that as you begin to work, too, that you're always looking forward to the mature church and what's going to be coming up later and how you're going to start from the very beginning, but then you want to continue to shape their thinking towards something that's true. So as we went through the culture and language learning, we kept note of their questions because they had lots of them and of course you can't answer them. They had to wait for the teaching and that was a long time—two years. So we kept a list of all the questions that they were asking. We promised them that the teaching that we're going to share does address every issue in our lives and that it can be used for every problem in our life, and so we would keep those questions and put a note at the end of the lesson where we could work that question in and their names. When we taught later, we were able to bring those questions back into the teaching and help them begin to judge the physical and material things and the concerns that they had with the Word of God.

As we were studying, there are three specific examples I can think of where we saw things in their culture that needed to be changed, but we weren't at a point where we'd earned the right to speak and we didn't have the Word of

God yet to stand on to make those changes.

One of the examples was in the area of education. They were being taken advantage of constantly by others out in town. They didn't understand money, counting or business and they were constantly being taken advantage of. They would hear stories from town that if you put money in the bank then it's going to just grow until you become a millionaire and you'll never have to worry about education again. They were just really pinning their hopes on these things and, time and time again, just being stolen from.

After the presentation we began to teach a class, educating them on what a bank is and what it looks like to make a fortnight and how to invest that and how to save their money. So as we're learning their culture we're always thinking long term how can we help them shape their worldview, not just through salvation, but then for their life and godliness.

One of the big things that we faced was that the witch doctors in the village were actually saying things to the people that in reality were killing the kids, like I mentioned before. Just one of the things they told them was when your kid gets sick, don't give them water. Water is bad. So people were coming to us with their kids dehydrated, to the point that there was no way for us to help so we actually just watched several kids die in our laps because we had no way to help them. That's really frustrating, because there's no reason this kid should die except for these rituals—rituals they've been told are going to save their kids, and they are actually killing their kids.

When they came to us, I used the example of a canoe. When a canoe is going under water and it's mostly full of water and ready to go underneath, it's too late to try to bail it out, and that's the way it was with the kids. They were bringing them to us right as they were dying and there was no way for us to help them so that was really heartbreaking and frustrating.

There're so many areas in animism where Satan's cutting away at their lives, at their marriages, at their family bonds. This was one of the ways, not taking medication, not drinking water, and after they became believers, we had said, drink water, you need to drink water. Then after they're believers, they'd come up and say, "Satan's been lying to us and we've been killing our own children." They were just realising the changes that will take place with the Gospel.

Before you even get to the point where you present the Gospel, your mindset should be to bring people on as a team to help you. We started looking for faithfulness in people who were actually being faithful to the work that we were asking them to do. The Lord was really good to us, because we saw that little bit of faithfulness in some, even before they were believers. And those men and women tend to be now the ones that are strong who are helping to lead the church on. I think it is really important to look for faithfulness, even before you present the Gospel, because those characteristics are something the Lord really used later on in their lives.

So overall, early on, there was a spirit of animism, a spirit of fear. They were fearful of everything, fearful that they when they went to the water they didn't wash properly, fearful that they ate something that they shouldn't have eaten, fearful to go by themselves to the garden, just in a constant spirit of fear in every aspect of their life.

In the later stages, that's what actually drew others into wanting to hear the Gospel. Others were looking at them and saw this lady going to the garden on her own and they're asking her, "Hey, are you going by yourself?" and she'd reply "Yes, He's with me. He's marked my day." So that's what attracted outsiders to the Gospel.

The whole story of the Gospel, from beginning to end, is just crucial in this whole process, but one of the stories that was really a tipping point of seeing where the people were moving, was the Tower of Babel, because the Tower of Babel, for the first time, explained how there were different people with different languages all over the world. They had a myth that they were spirits actually coming back to us. When they heard that story, the Lord used that powerfully to change their whole mindset to realise, "Oh, they're just people. They're not spirits." So that was a story that the Lord used to really empower and change the thinking of a lot of people, which led them to believe the story as it started to unfold.

As they heard the Gospel, many believed and the church was born and they started meeting. One of the big things was the whole idea of being brought in through baptism, abiding with the body through communion, elders being raised up eventually and then looking out beyond their own borders to the villages next to them where they had family, and that all came from the book of Acts really. They started walking through the book of Acts and realising the church met together and grew together, then it went out into the community, and so that's the model they followed.

We really didn't push them into any of those things. We just kept teaching the Word of God and making sure that we were pointing out the fact that this is a message that is to be taken out to others. It has meaning in your own life and then it is supposed to spill out into your other relationships, and the church has really done that. One of the things that we've seen over the years is the Lord growing the church and strengthening the church by making it smaller.

Because we were in that animistic context where everybody was looking for something and so everybody latched on to it, it's taken many years to get to the point to where the people who were just holding onto the Gospel for the sake of what they could get out of it for themselves are starting to fall away. It's leaving this mature, strong body, smaller (and it's kind of sad to see that when you see some of your friends walk away from the Gospel) but a solid group that is the church and doing really well. They're feeding themselves and growing together in their context and that's where the church is right now.

The day that we started to present the Gospel, we had two little girls, aged five and seven, and they had been part of our team and very supportive and excited about bringing the Gospel to this people group. That morning we got out little mustard seeds and we taped them on the front of their Bibles and we told them that we're trusting the Lord, like this little mustard seed, to do work here. Then we walked out the door, all nervous, for our first day. Everybody's going to be talking about these spiritual things that we've been so excited to bring.

We walk down and pray with our co-workers and get to the trail where the trail begins to narrow. Right in the middle of the trail, there's a snake and its head has been crushed. Somebody came by with a pole or a post or something and crushed his head and it's just laying right there in the trail. We just all stopped and thought, "Yeah, this battle is the Lord's. He's the one building this church and this little mustard seed, it's going to grow. It's not dependent on us; it's the Spirit of God."

To see them now on the other end, elders who are discerning and kind and merciful and full of wisdom and able to lead—they've gone from fear and death to these leadership qualities that God promises—we know that it's just His Word. It's prayer and it's the Spirit and Him that will get His work done.

All the snapshots above represent a wide range of contexts and a lot of different challenges. We will continue to see what we can learn from these different case studies and how the WILD framework applies to them. It will help us make what can be actually quite an ambiguous process a lot more concrete as we start to see some of these patterns unfold and how these different church planters, through God's wisdom and through His Word, are able to apply the things that they were learning from Scripture.

We'll explore God's intent for these churches and see that process unfold in their individual contexts.

DISCUSSION POINTS

1. As you listen to the contexts described in this tutorial, use the following headings to note anything that you think could have been a significant barrier to the Gospel.
- Physical
- Linguistic
- Cultural
- Relational
- Other challenges related to the country or context

2. A comment was made in the video that it is easy to lose sight of the long-term goals of church planting in the context. What do you imagine are some of the possible consequences of not keeping overall goals in sight?

ACTIVITIES

1. Research and in a short paragraph describe 'Buddhism'. Note down your sources of information. (You will find a 3-part video series on Buddhism at AccessTruth.com)

9.3 Access to the Bible

✓ OBJECTIVES OF THIS TUTORIAL

This tutorial discusses the first question in the area of Word: 'Are they able to access the Bible in a form that clearly and faithfully communicates God's revelation to them?'

Matthew 28:18-20: Jesus came and told his disciples, "I have been given all authority in heaven and on earth. Therefore, go and make disciples of all the nations, baptizing them in the name of the Father and the Son and the Holy Spirit. Teach these new disciples to obey all the commands I have given you. And be sure of this: I am with you always, even to the end of the age." (New Living Translation)

Looking at those verses above in light of the session, we see a reference to the Great Commission, a commission for all God's children to be disciplemakers. But in order for us to be able to do that we have to have God's Word in a way that we can understand for ourselves so that we can communicate it clearly to others. To do that cross-culturally is very challenging. Those who are wanting to teach need to be able to hear it, understand it, and then be able to, in turn, pass it on. To be disciple-makers, people need to have His Word. It's quite a simple concept but it actually becomes an incredible challenge to the work. It's refreshing that He says that He's with us in that. That's our authority and also the way that we're empowered to do it.

Last Time

We looked at some snapshots of the cross-cultural church planting scenarios we will be focusing on during this Module. In this tutorial we will look at the first question in the WILD outline and hear from some experienced church planters on how this area impacts their work.

Are they able to access the Bible in a form that clearly and faithfully communicates God's revelation to them?

Kaikou talks about their first experience of hearing God's Word clearly taught:

> In the past, we thought we understood who the Creator was, but we were just in darkness. But we now understand the plan that God had to bring His Word to us. Some foreigners came to live among us and they learned our language and culture. At that time, they realized that we thought we knew about God, but the reality was that we knew nothing about God. During that time, they began to ask us questions like, "Where do you think animals came from originally?" And we didn't have a good clear answer for that. Another question that was raised during that time was, "What actually happens to a person when they die?"
>
> In answering that question, we gave many different responses. We didn't have one clear answer. All of that helped to prepare us for God's Word, and for us to sense our real need. So when the time came when they began to share God's Word with us, our hearts had been prepared beforehand, because it was clear to us that there were many important things that we needed to understand. So when we heard God's Word in our own true language, we understood it clearly and it revealed many things that we had previously been confused about.

Gebi adds to what Kaikou said, specifically talking about hearing God's Word in their own language:

> Before, we only had the Bible in the national language, but the message just did not speak to our hearts. Then, we heard God's Word in our own specific language, explained clearly from the beginning, and so it made sense. We heard it like that and then we were in awe of God as He described Himself. We understood God's character and His intentions towards us as human beings.

Do they feel as though it's God Himself speaking to them through the Bible when they hear or read it, OR does the language tend to create barriers and give the idea that it is for someone else?

Dave talks about their experience of providing access to a natural, clear translation of God's Word:

> It gave us great pleasure to be able to take God's Word to the people we worked among, and give it to them in their own language, something that they had never had. And when we translated God's Word, we wanted to be sure that it spoke the language that they speak. We wanted to make sure that it truly represented the meaning of the source texts, but we also wanted to

make sure that it spoke in a way that was clearly understandable to them and even sounded natural, to sound like the way they speak.

Phil explained how significant it is when people connect God's narrative to the real events of their lives:

> As we're teaching the story, we're wanting them to fit themselves into that story. And the degree to which we see them fitting themselves into the story that we're teaching from God's Word is the degree to which their identity becomes guided by the things that they're learning from God's Word. To us, that's where the progress is. So, for instance, when some guy comes to me and says, "Oh, you're struggling with our language today. You're tripping up on stuff." He's like "Man, God did a really good job there in Babel when he mixed up all those languages." And I'm thinking to myself, Bingo. They're interpreting something that happens to them today from something that they've heard from God's Word. They're recognising that this is affecting us today, whether it's sin—"Man, Adam and Eve really messed it up"—and looking at some situation. I'm thinking to myself, Bingo. You're relating this terrible thing that happened in the community to Adam and Eve's sin."

Does the language they are hearing the Truth in give them the ability to talk about it in their homes, with their friends, and in the community?

Clark talks about the significant difference since the group they work with have had Scripture translated in their own language:

> When we first moved in, and we first started teaching, it was pretty much an oral presentation of the Gospel. We worked off lessons, but didn't have any Scripture that we were using. If we did use Scripture, it was the Thai Scriptures. We started Bible translation about eight or nine years into the church plant. The people don't have a real desire for God's Word in their own language, they can read Thai, but we've found as we've translated, the more we've translated the more they've appreciated having God's Word in their own language. And we've seen the effect of that on the church has been more of an understanding. We've seen more growth the more we've had it in their own language.

Greg talks about the process of learning culture and language and the depth of understanding needed to share the Truth clearly in that setting:

> When arriving in the country, as we began developing relationships, one of the first things we did was to begin to understand how they saw the world, what they valued in the world, and what was lacking in their understanding

of who God is and how God impacts them and their society. We began by taking time to discuss with them and by asking questions like what do they see in the world? How do they perceive the world? What do they value? We began to learn a lot about what communism had brought in and what even this new view of Buddhism was. They had a very limited view of God. They had a very superstitious view in the way they understood the world. They were very strong in this idea that they could somehow manipulate society by luck or by chance. And we began to understand a little bit better about how they perceive the world around them.

Even though it was a communist society, my perception of that meant, at the time, that they didn't believe in anything spiritual—that they had no spiritual values—and that wasn't true. They actually had a pretty strong spiritual perception of the world, although they could hold an atheistic view. They didn't see it as a dichotomy that they would have somehow a perception of being atheist, they believed they could be atheist and also believe in a god or believe in a million gods as in Buddhism. We found that there could be all kinds of contradictions for them.

Matt talks about their situation in which house-to-house teaching is important:

Our strategies or our focus in teaching our friends who wanted to be taught, or were open to being taught in their homes was teaching foundationally from Creation to Christ. And at this point, due to their work schedule and their lifestyle, we are able to teach three to four times a month in this situation, so it takes us a considerable amount of time to work our way through the teaching with them.

We've made adjustments to our teaching because the people have exposure to the Catholic church and exposure to other churches in our area; they have an understanding of some of the content of the Scripture, but they have no understanding of the meaning of that content. And so one of the things we did recently with this family is we, in our first conversation together, gave them a panoramic view of where the story is going. So we started in creation and we, very quickly in one session, went through to Christ coming back in the future. And that has really helped us with them—to help keep them on the storyline and where we're at when we're teaching the Bible. It helps them relate to what they're hearing in the story, how that relates to when Jesus lived and when they are living, and to keep it straight on the storyline and in line with history.

Are they able to access God's Word in the available media and technologies that the wider society is using?

Greg talks about the communication challenges in their work among the deaf community:

> It was a process of developing sign language. We were in the process of working with some of the educated leaders in the deaf community, developing ways to express those thoughts in sign language, and even to be able to describe that literacy was a problem amongst deaf people. We had to work with them in the area of literacy, helping them understand how to read, how to understand the Bible, how to understand God's Word and what it meant for them. That was a big challenge for most of them. Much of the Bible was difficult for them to get or grasp. Even though they might have understood the word or been able to spell the word, to understand the depth of meaning of it, we had to teach this idea of what it means, a meaning-based understanding of God's Word.

Dave talks about the importance of literacy and how it has impacted the lives of the people:

> Along with giving them the translated Scriptures, of course, we had to teach them how to read and write their own language, which they had never done before. We produced a literacy course of several booklets that we took several of the adults through and eventually trained literacy teachers. It's still ongoing today. There are literacy teachers there that are teaching literacy, teaching more of the people how to read and write their own language. We knew that some of the older people would never learn how to read and write their own language, but that was okay.

> We found that with the people we worked with, when they read the Scriptures or when they read anything really, they pretty much always read aloud. It's like it never occurred to them to just look at the words and just think them because when they speak, they're speaking aloud, so when they read, they read aloud. Often, someone will be sitting in a house and they'll be reading Scripture aloud and other people will gather around and start to listen. We also encouraged the younger ones, the ones who were able to learn how to read, to read the Scriptures aloud to their parents and grandparents, as some of them were perhaps at the age where it would have been very, very difficult for them to learn how to read. It didn't really matter because they could hear the Scriptures being read regularly by their children and grandchildren.

ACCESS TO THE BIBLE

Matt explains some of the ways they are equipping the church:

> We view ourselves as assisting the believers in any way we can through teaching, discipleship, and developing more curriculum. One of our biggest projects right now is to bring the written curriculum into an audio form so that we can get more people listening to the Word, listening to the teaching. And so those are just different ways we want to assist.

We started off this session with the Great Commission in Matthew 28. As disciples, the goal is to make more disciples of Christ. In order for them to become disciples of Christ, they need to know God's Word and not just at a surface level, but actually know Him in deep ways. And that requires being familiar with God's Word to the point that it impacts their lives, to the point where they become disciples of Christ who in turn can make more disciples of Christ. It's quite a high level of Bible-literacy that is required to be able to achieve in-depth understanding. We need to make every effort so that others can have access to God's Word and the ability to know it, and then to know Him through it, and then to help others to do the same.

 DISCUSSION POINTS

1. As you watch the tutorial video, note any reasons given for the importance of having the Bible in a language that clearly communicates.

2. Reflect on any connection that you can see between:

- A community having access to a Bible translation that is both accurate and natural, and
- God's Word becoming a part of people's everyday lives rather than just a religious manuscript.

 ACTIVITIES

1. Research the concept of 'High Religion/Low Religion'. Note down three or four contrasting characteristics of 'High Religion' and 'Low Religion'.

This week try to talk with two people who might use a Bible in more than one language. Prepare a few questions beforehand to ask them about

TUTORIAL 9.3

Bible translations or versions in languages they understand (include questions about:languages they speak, preferences for Bible translation for personal use, etc.). Note your questions and the responses you get.

9.4 Engaging at a worldview level

 OBJECTIVES OF THIS TUTORIAL

This tutorial discusses the first question in the area of Word: 'Are they able to access the Bible in a form that clearly and faithfully communicates God's revelation to them?'

Hebrews 4:12: For the word of God is alive and powerful. It is sharper than the sharpest two-edged sword, cutting between soul and spirit, between joint and marrow. It exposes our innermost thoughts and desires.

That verse is quite appropriate as we think about God's Word and the inherent power of His Word in this tutorial. He's wanting us to be able to hear His Word so that its power can penetrate. It doesn't work if we have a copy of it in a language that we don't understand. It's important to actually have it in a format that we can understand, that the way it's communicated in our language is clear and so able to actually divide all the way to the innermost part of our selves and do what God intends for it to do. God's Word enters not only into hearts but also into a community as well and cuts right into it.

Last time

We looked at the first question from the WILD outline. We talked about many issues relating to people having access to a clear and faithful translation of God's Word.

In this tutorial we will discuss the second question in the WILD outline which is also in the area of Word.

Are they having God's Word presented to them in a way that allows it to enter and engage their hearts at a worldview level?

Are those sharing Truth with them taking the responsibility seriously; are they qualified, gifted and equipped for that particular setting, and are they genuinely committed to getting to know and understand the worldview of those they're sharing with?

Greg talks about the absolute need to build relationships in a suspicious, former Soviet republic:

> We began by building relationships, taking the time to get to know the people. It was very important for us to build a bridge for them through relationships. The suspicion that they had for us as foreigners was huge. They thought that one of our objectives was to somehow overthrow their government. It was very early on that a deep level of distrust was taking place, so one of the challenges that we had was to try to grow in our understanding of their culture, to grow in our understanding of what they did, to try to talk to them about aspects of God; that God actually does exist and how God can impact their lives and that there is truth.

Greg talks about the efforts they made to become good communicators in the language of the community they lived in:

> The language we learned was a Russian language. That was the heart language of the people that we were working with. To understand the language, to be able to communicate clearly with them, that took time. For us we had the extra challenge of not only the people group that we were working with, but also with the deaf community. We began to learn their language. It was interesting to us that although you could have a complete society of deaf people living within a Russian culture of the time, they could have completely different cultures. Dealing with the Russians and dealing with the deaf were completely different. Their worldview is very different. Having to learn their language allowed us to be able to understand better how they saw the world, who they are in this world, and actually show them that we cared about them enough to learn their language clearly enough to communicate with them. When they had struggles, we could deal with it. When they had questions, we could answer those questions because we were able to speak both those languages.

Dave talks about how important it is for Bible teachers to understand the worldview of those they are teaching:

> Well, it was very important that we had learned their worldview (the way they viewed the world around them) because, of course, it's from that perspective that they would receive everything that we told them. The fact that we understood their view of the spiritual forces and of the spirit beings that were floating all around them meant that we were able to present truth in a way that they would understand. There were many parts of their culture that we were able to use to help them better understand the truths of the Gospel.

One of the areas that really proved to be helpful and beneficial is their court system. They have their own ways of dealing with wrongs within their society. It's not the same as ours, but there are three main elements to their court system that really made a good outline for presenting the Gospel.

First of all, they understand that when a wrong has been done, payment must be made. For example, if someone steals something or if adultery is committed or if they injure someone intentionally or kill someone, payment must be made. As long as payment has not been made, the offended parties have nothing to do with each other. They won't look at each other. They won't come near each other. Obviously, they will not speak to each other. Fellowship between them is completely cut off. Now, some people in our society would suggest that there's a balance system that perhaps if my good deeds outweigh my bad deeds, then surely God will accept me.

From their perspective, they understand that this doesn't make sense because as long as a deed has not been paid for, fellowship is broken and things are not back to what they should be until payment of some kind has been made. Even in our own culture, we understand that payment must be made. Say, for example, there was a doctor who, through his medical practice, saved the lives of a thousand people. Then at one point, he murdered one person. Well, I guess we'd say, "That's okay. I mean, he only killed one person, but he saved a thousand." So that should be okay, right? His good deeds outweigh his bad deeds. Well, even in secular society people realise that this doesn't make sense. When that doctor stands trial for murdering that one person, the fact that he saved a thousand lives is totally irrelevant. The people we worked amongst clearly understood that.

A second aspect to their court system is that they understand that when a wrong has been done, first payment must be made—but it must be the right payment. It must be the payment that is prescribed by the village elders, and generally that would include strings of shell money. If it's a serious crime it might also include live pigs, which are very, very valuable to them. They're domestic pigs. We said, "Well, what if a person said, 'I don't have any shell money. I don't have any pigs, so I'll give you something else. Maybe I'll give you a shirt or something else.'" They said, "No. That would not do." If the offending party doesn't have the right payment, he needs to get it from his relatives, from his brothers and uncles. They need to help him make this payment. It has to be the right payment. If you try to give the offended party the wrong payment, the offence will grow even greater. They understand that it must be the right payment.

Of course, we know from Scripture that there is only one payment for the sin debt that we all have and that is the blood of Jesus Christ when he died on the cross at Calvary. The third important element to their court system is once payment has been made, it's a dead issue. They will never bring it up again. It's something I think they understand perhaps even better than we do. If a wrong has been done the village elders came together, they agree on the payment, and once the payment has been made and accepted no one will bring that issue up again. It will never be discussed again. If you bring that issue up after the payment has been made and accepted, now there's going to be another court case. Now you are in trouble because you brought up this issue that had already been paid for.

Is God's Word being shared with them in a way that gives the Spirit opportunity to "prepare the soil" by challenging fundamental assumptions, commitments and alignments?

Dave talks about how the animistic worldview was challenged in the community where they lived in the time before they taught God's Word:

Initially, when we were learning their language and culture, we just wanted to be learners. We didn't seriously question any of their beliefs early on because we wanted them to be open and honest and tell us everything that they believed. Then, as we got closer to the time that we were going to be teaching them God's truth, we did begin asking them questions about some of their beliefs; how they believed it was their own personal power that was controlling the rain and the growth of food in their gardens. It was their own personal power that controlled sicknesses. For example, there were certain individuals in our village who claimed to be rainmakers and we said, "There are places in the world where it almost never rains and if you could produce rain and go to that place, perhaps the Sahara in Africa, and produce rain there, then they would pay you a lot of money."

Some of them started to understand the fact that some of these beliefs, perhaps, didn't really fit with reality. Also, when they would talk about sorcery, they would talk about tying up a person's spirit and then eventually that it would squeeze the life out of that person and that person would eventually die. We started asking questions about that, too, as they understood that God is the Creator and so He's the Creator of human spirits. Can we really tie up another person's spirit that God has created? They started to question some of the beliefs. I remember early on in our teaching, when we were asking questions about some of these beliefs, and afterwards, hearing some of them discussing these things and starting to realise that, wow, the things that their ancestors had told them didn't all really make sense. Their belief that they had held onto without question was starting to unravel. It was encouraging to see the truth of God's Word do this.

Dave gives a description of the way they taught in order to address the worldview in its most foundational elements:

Once we had learned their language and culture well enough to communicate the truths of God's Word to them, we wanted to find out from them when would be the best times to teach and what's the best time of year with their gardening cycle. We worked all that out with them and initially taught them five days a week for about 45 minutes per session. We started at the very beginning of the Bible, first establishing the authority of God's Word and then getting into who God is. We started teaching in Genesis chapter one with Creation. We hit the high points through the Old Testament and, eventually, the life of Christ. It took several months before we eventually presented them the truth of the Gospel—salvation through Jesus Christ alone. At that point, a small church was born.

John talks about how he and Betty and the rest of their team contributed to the preparation for God's Word through their lives:

So anyway, one day I was talking with a couple of guys and I started to tell them that we'd actually come with a message. It was great that we could help them medically and honestly, I believe the medical program was a tremendous tool for building relationships and developing that trust. That was a very tangible way of showing them that we really did care about them and building those relationships. But I said to them, "It's been great that we could do that, it's been great that we could do some things to help you economically as well, but there's another reason we came and that's the most important reason. We've come with a message, and the One who made everything that you see around you wants you to know His Story. That's why we've left our families back in Australia and America and Chris and Ida have left their families and come here to live amongst you, and we've spent all this time learning your language. It's so that we can tell you this Story."

Now by this time, they knew that we were Christians, and they were pretty wary of that, but somehow I think God had been at work building these relationships and we'd been hard at work too. So I think they were fairly confident that we were on their side, that we were there for them, we cared about them and we'd had ample opportunity to show them love. They had seen that the things that scared the daylights out of them didn't scare us, and that had a huge impact on them.

In fact, one woman said to my wife, "Why aren't you leaving the house when your neighbours die because his spirit is going to come back and get even with anyone who's offended him. We're all taking off and you need to take off too." And Betty said, "No, we're just going to stay. We're not afraid." The woman said, "Why aren't you afraid?" And Betty said, "Well, that's the real reason we've come here to live amongst you and are learning your language, so that we can tell you that.' "This woman said to Betty, "Oh, I hope you learn our language quickly, because we want to know that." There were lots of little incidents that I think had them thinking, "There's more to this than what we can see." When the time was right, we started what we call pre-evangelism, starting to prepare the people for the coming story.

In this setting John and Betty had opportunity to teach God's Word to a large group for an extended period of time:

And come they did, about 250 of them turned up every Monday, Wednesday and Friday. The majority of those stuck right through for six months, the six months that it took us to work our way through the Old Testament. We spent four months on the Old Testament and about two months on the life of Christ. As we progressively unfolded God's story—that's what we called it, God's story—we just saw God do an amazing work amongst those people as His truth penetrated that darkness and illuminated their minds. For the first time, they heard the truth that there was a God who made them and who cared about them enough to send Someone to make sure they understood all He had done to redeem them. I think that period of my life was probably the most exciting six months ever. It was an incredible privilege of just witnessing God at work among a people who knew nothing of Him, and who, for the first time, had the opportunity to find out.

Greg discusses the challenges of getting down to a worldview level in a deaf community:

Literacy was a problem amongst deaf people so we had to work with them in the area of literacy, helping them understand how to read, how to understand the Bible, how to understand God's Word and what it meant for them. It was a big challenge for most of them. Much of the Bible was difficult for them to grasp. Even though they might've understood the word or been able to spell the word, to understand the depth of its meaning meant we had to teach this idea of what it means, a meaning-based understanding of God's Word. Amongst the Russians, and amongst the people group we worked with especially, they used a very different vocabulary from what was in the Bible, what was in God's Word, so actually helping them understand it from God's perspective and having them understand a different worldview was challenging.

Phil gives a cultural example of some of the commitments and alignments that need to be challenged:

> Here's one of the illustrations that we used. They have divorce. You can divorce your wife and there's a little symbolic coin, like a small amount of money that you would give publicly to your wife, or the wife gives to the husband, depending on the situation, where it's like a final divorce saying, "We divorced." You can divorce, but nobody's free to marry somebody else until this symbolic little coin is handed over and now it's over.
>
> We're saying, "What happens when, as a woman, this guy you know has divorced this lady over here and he comes over to you and he's telling you that he really loves you and he wants to marry you and you've got his whole heart and he's committed to you and nobody else, but you know for a fact that he's never severed completely this tie over here with this woman. He's still holding his back door open that says that he can go back to her at any time. What does that tell you as a woman if he's saying he's totally committed to you but he actually hasn't severed ties over here?"
>
> They're like, "Yeah. He's just lying. He's a …" They've got a word for one of those guys who cheats and takes advantage of women. They're like, "That's what it is." We're saying we trust God, but in our back pocket we've got kind of this backdoor openness kind of thing where we can get out of this and we actually trust a few other things.
>
> We're trying to work with them, saying God's intent for us is total commitment and total rest in His sufficiency and what He's done on the cross. We're seeing guys as they understand and hearing it in their conversations, their prayers and the discussions and the teaching. I think it was always there for a lot of those guys, that they really did only trust Him and they realized this right from the beginning, but we're hearing this growing sense from them as a corporate identity, "We are people who trust only in what God did through Christ. That's what distinguishes us from the people around us, because the people around us are trusting what they've done. We're trusting in what Christ has done for us. It's not what we bring to the table in terms of, 'Here, God. Accept me for this reason.' We're coming empty handed and saying, 'It's what Christ has done for us.'"

> Is Truth being shared with them in a way that leads them to stand honestly and humbly before God and to turn to Jesus Christ as God's answer to their deepest longings and needs?

Greg gives an example of a situation in which a high level of education proved to be a barrier to be overcome:

> We were working with a people group that's actually considered one of the largest people groups in the country that we were working in, but the most unreached group in the area. A lot of times when people think of people groups, they have a perspective of uneducated or village-type situations. Although they may have lived in villages, the education level for these guys was astronomical. There were more PhDs amongst the people group that we worked with than any other ethnic group probably in Russia. Just to say that, there are probably more educated Russians than other group in the world, so it's almost safe to say that they're one of the highest educated people groups in the world of academics. There are astronauts, there are people that've created all sorts of things. They're very artistic. They're very good in science.
>
> When we were working with them, their understanding of literacy and teaching them how to read wasn't our issue. It was hard for them to understand about who God is. Their ability to take what they've understood and actually reach into the community has been phenomenal to see. Today it's a very different society than it was 20 years ago.

Kaikou explains how key it was for them to engage with Bible teaching in their heart language so it spoke to the deeper areas of their existing worldview:

> Previously, when we heard anything about the Bible, it was in the national language and it didn't really communicate to us. Then, when we heard God's Word in our own language, it entered right into our lives and God was revealed to us through his Word. In the very language that was used and in the underlying meaning that came through, we realised that God's Word was true. Before it was in the language of others, but now we saw it as our own.
>
> Just as an example, it's like when we eat from another place, it just doesn't taste as good as the food grown in our own gardens. When we eat the food grown in our own soil, it is the most satisfying. I'm referring to the difference between hearing in the national language or hearing in our own language. Hearing it in the national language just doesn't taste as good to us and it is just not clear. Hearing it in our own language revealed the underlying things

in our culture, like superstitions and traditions and our own self-efforts. It made those things clear and it showed us the way of faith in Christ. We realised there was nothing we could do. Our own efforts were useless. The only way to be restored to God is through Jesus Christ and what he did on our behalf. We clearly understood the true way of God after having heard His Word in our own language.

Philip talks about the need for clear, heart-level teaching so people truly understand the work of Christ:

> A very important factor was hearing God's Word in our own language rather than in the trade language. For example, the issue of sin and God's judgement on sin was not clear to us before. Once we learned in our own language about who God is and what He's like, we realised that we owed a debt for our sin and that we would be judged for that. Then we were prepared to hear that God had provided the payment for that through the Saviour. We understood the good news that God had sent Him to deal with the debt of sin that we couldn't pay for.

The testimonies in this tutorial bring home the need to have God's Word presented in a way that allows it to enter and engage. The verse at the beginning of this tutorial reminds us that God's Word is a powerful, sharp, two-edged sword that He's fashioned to cut deep into the hearts of people and into communities. We've seen the importance of those who wield that sword to engage at a worldview level: understanding the culture, knowing language well, going the extra mile, understanding the situation in the context so the sword goes in and does the work, penetrating and exposing people's hearts and their pride and doing what God intends for it to do.

ENGAGING AT A WORLDVIEW LEVEL

? DISCUSSION POINTS

1. In the video there was strong support given for living in a community long-term. In your view is that always necessary for church planting goals to be reached, or are other more short-term approaches sometimes appropriate? Explain your thinking.

2. Picture yourself in a conversation with a friend who expresses the strong view that it isn't necessary for a Bible teacher to spend years learning the language or understanding the culture and worldview assumptions of his/her audience. How would you respond to them?

3. Many people living in cross-cultural situations are faced at some point with confronting religious or cultural practices. Imagine what might be some of the long-term implications of either avoiding or getting too involved in those kinds of situations.

9.5 The authority of God's word

✓ OBJECTIVES OF THIS TUTORIAL

This tutorial discusses the third question in the area of Word: 'Are they learning to give God's Word its proper place and authority?'

2 Corinthians 10:4-5: We use God's mighty weapons, not worldly weapons, to knock down the strongholds of human reasoning and to destroy false arguments. We destroy every proud obstacle that keeps people from knowing God. We capture their rebellious thoughts and teach them to obey Christ.

Those verse are a reminder that the enemy uses tactics to give false arguments. He raised himself up in pride and was rebellious. In a lot of the contexts that we find ourselves serving where God is wanting us to bring His truth, we find that people are actually prepared against the Gospel. Yet God says here that He's able to tear down these barriers and it's through the authority of God's Word.

Last time

We looked at the second question from the WILD outline. We focused on the way that God's Word is presented to people and how that effects whether it truly engages them at a worldview level. In this tutorial we will discuss the third question in the WILD outline which is also in the area of Word.

Are they learning to give God's Word its proper place and authority?

We asked Clark, "What are the primary voices in the community? And therefore what were the primary voices for those who are now the believers in that area?" He replied:

> The authority that the people would have had when we moved in would've been primarily their family unit. Elders and uncles would've been the ones that would have spoken into their lives the most. Another big voice would've been peers. Friends are extremely important, so they'd have been looking for their peers' approval. They would have been a huge voice in their life. Secondary to that would've been the national Thai culture, school teachers,

that type of thing. Those were the voices that they would have been listening to.

Phil talks about how they positioned themselves as religious teachers in the community and how that played out in terms of the authority of God's Word there:

> As we were coming into this community, first we're put in the category of rich foreigners because we've got cars and generators. What we're working towards is becoming known as people who, first of all, walk uprightly in terms of the local way of understanding walking uprightly; that we're people who are qualified to talk about religion. We have conversations about it constantly with people, and so there's a sense of authority. We know what we're talking about, and we can actually enter into these conversations.
>
> Even in the Islamic side, for me personally, having read lots and lots of the history, you're driving down the road and you're turning to your Muslim guys and you're like, "Do you know who Hamsa was in relation to the prophet and how he worked with the prophet to protect him, and also to give him authority and to give him prestige? Because Hamsa, there was a supporter behind him." And they're like, "How do you know this stuff about Hamsa if you're not Muslim?" And if there's a question about Catholicism, we're answering why things happen the way they do. So, by lots and lots of different conversations in the realm of religion, we're building the sense that we understand quite a bit of what God's Word says and what the history is, and how all these different religions tie together. So we're building this identity along the way of, I guess you'd call it, authority, in religious topics, while trying to maintain a sense of independence about it without committing to one side or the other. If we're going to commit to anything, we're going to commit to who God is and what He says, and that's what we're trying to follow.

Are those sharing Truth with them keenly aware of the battle, and is that causing them to humbly depend on God and to lean on others in the Body for encouragement, input and accountability?

Clark explains some of the obstacles they encountered and the answers they have found in seeing the authority of God's Word established there:

> I would say of God's Word becoming authority...and I'll be brutally honest here; when we moved in, we didn't really understand the voices, or even the authority that we were trying to give God's Word. So it wasn't a huge part of our initial presentation of the Gospel, and we didn't recognise what was

happening as far as us as foreigners going in there. The people are very much looking for an advantage over their peers, and having a foreigner come in and live on their land was a huge step up in their minds. So there was a lot of stuff going on in that area, where they were looking at anything that the foreigner was presenting as a way of getting ahead economically, which we didn't recognise initially.

I believe when we did teach them the first few times, they came to faith in Christ. But they made decisions very early on that they were going to become whatever it was that we laid out. It wasn't an understanding of truth with God's Word being the authority. And that left some very weak foundations in the church. I would say in the last couple years we've had more translated material to give to them and actually are teaching from God's Word. It's radically changed how we teach. Rather than having to spend most of our time in the teaching saying, "This is what God's Word says," we can actually read it, and then I would illustrate it by shining a light on what is actually being said in the Scriptures. I think they're finally starting to see that the authority is God's Word, not the missionary, not the teacher that's out there speaking. Probably where we've started to really see a growth taking place, in light of that, was when we taught through First Corinthians, and they say that this is what God's Word says. It actually challenged them and they made some radical changes in how they behaved and thought about it.

Is Truth being shared with them so that it's answering the big questions of life while also being relevant to their everyday concerns; and are their felt needs being addressed in light of people's real needs before God?

We asked Greg how the authority of God's Word was established in an area that was formerly part of the Soviet system:

> One of the biggest challenges we found early on was this failure in the idea that there was any kind of truth that existed at all, and we actually began to go back to the very basics of helping them just to decide, "Is there such a thing as truth?" Is there something that they can believe in? Is there something that's knowable out there that they didn't understand?

Dave reflects on how the authority of God's Word grew and challenged animistic beliefs:

> From the very start when we began teaching them God's Word, we told them, "We're not going to tell you our ideas. We're not going to tell you anyone else's ideas. We are going to tell you what God says. Everything that we say is going to be based on what is in the Scriptures, what is in this book, The

Bible." They clearly understood that before we even got into the early narratives of the Old Testament, and we saw the authority of God's Word at work in their lives, even in areas that we had not specifically targeted and explicitly told them about.

I remember one time, I went out to a garden with one of my local friends, and there was this large elephant ear-like plant that they were deathly afraid of. We learned that early on when we were making the airstrip. I remember one time, I was out there working with them, and I was about to cut some down, and it was at the time that my wife was expecting our first child, and they said, "No, no! Don't cut that down! Your wife is pregnant, and the child will die!"

I could've just said, "Well, I don't believe in that phoney belief," and I could've just cut it down. But what if my wife had had a miscarriage? That would've confirmed in their minds that their belief was true, or even if she hadn't, they would've just thought that perhaps I had some kind of strong magical power to be able to overcome the deadly effects of this plant. So I stepped aside and they sent an older woman over there. Her children were grown and it wasn't a danger for her.

Well, then several years later after we had taught them the Scriptures and there was a church established there in our village, I went out to a garden with one of the men, and he was clearing this area, and he came upon some of this plant, and he just cut it all down. And I knew that his wife had just had a baby that week, a tiny, tiny infant, and that's when the children are the most susceptible and when this plant would cause the pre-born or newly born child to die. And we had never specifically talked about this in our teaching, and so I said, "I thought you guys were afraid of that plant." And he said, "Oh, we used to be, but we don't have to be afraid of the spirit of that plant anymore. We know that God's Spirit is much more powerful than that." And it was encouraging to see that God was working in their hearts even beyond the specific things that we were telling them, that the authority of God's Word was making changes in areas of their lives that we had not even targeted.

An example from Mexico of a man who was processing the authority of religious figures in contrast to God's true authority:

Recently, the pope visited Mexico, and it was a big event. Everyone was talking about his visit, and the people group we worked among wrestle with whether or not they're Catholic. They don't really believe they're Catholic, but the government tells them they're Catholic, and the Catholic church tells them they're Catholic. So, in our teaching time, my friend Crus was asking me about the pope and who he was. I was trying to explain to him that the pope is the leader of this religion, and the people in that religion follow what he says, and he speaks for God. He speaks on behalf of God to that religion. And Cruz, in his very demonstrative, playful way, was joking about how the pope, if he was a man, then he was a sinner just like Cruz. And being a sinner, there's no way that he could speak for God, because no sinner could speak for God.

We were just listening to him, and so I asked Cruz, "So, Cruz, who could speak for God?" And he said, "There's only One who lived perfectly and who could speak for God, and that's Jesus Christ. I'm going to listen to Him. I'm going to listen to what He has to say, because He's the only One that could speak for God." We were probably in the lesson of Abraham and Isaac at that point when he was processing that. So we continued to work through the stories using foundational Bible teaching with these guys, and allowed for their questions and their understanding to grow, but we continue to keep working from the storyline, and we're excited because we're seeing a growing understanding in this family's minds and hearts of who Jesus Christ is, and why He came.

Gebi relates an incident of an untimely death that initially unsettled the community of believers:

An example of God's work becoming the authority in our community life was when someone died. A woman died suddenly, and it was a huge shock to everyone. It caused tension in the community, as these kinds of sudden tragedies always did in our culture. But then we remembered that God is in control of all things, including death, and the believers were convinced that God is the One in charge, and so that settled things and dispelled the tensions in the community.

Kaikou explains more about the implications of that particular situation:

In the past, when there was a sudden death in our village, it would create enormous conflict. Houses would even be destroyed in the fighting. Then we understood the true origins of death, and that it was a direct result of sin. When we had that, we chose to believe God's Word and what it says about life and death. And now there are no longer huge tensions and conflict when someone dies. One part of this is that there is a real respect for the leaders that God has put into place, and people listen to them as well.

Are they aligning their lives to God's Word, not from fear, but as a result of understanding more of God's grace and a growing assurance of salvation?

John describes how God's Word brought about freedom in place of the fears people had lived with:

> I think there's no doubt about the fact that the method of evangelism, teaching foundationally and starting in Genesis where God starts, it just made sense. It made the picture so much clearer for the people. I said to them, "It's like telling a story. We don't tell a story and begin halfway through. So we're going to start this story right back in the beginning." And as we did that, the amazing thing was, after we taught the story of the fall and God's promise in Genesis 3:15, that we said to the people, "Okay, we're going to cease teaching here, because we know that it's the time of year when you all go off and do your spirit festival. We're just going to wait for you to do that, come back, and then we'll recommence, because we don't want you to miss any part of the story. We know a lot of you will go away to do that, so we'll wait till you return."
>
> One of the guys said to me, "Well, we're not going away this year. In fact, we're probably never going to go away again. In fact, we've taken our spirit rocks that we travel with and depend upon for safety, and we've crushed them up, and we've thrown them in the river. We've taken our other fetishes that we believe protect us, and we've thrown them in the river, and they're all washed out to sea now, so we'll never get them back." And I said, "Why did you do that?"—Because we had never condemned any of that. We were very careful not to change their lifestyle. We wanted God's Word to bring about that change, and not conformity to what we wanted to see, or what we thought was right.
>
> So I said to him, "Why did you do that? What made you do that? And why aren't you going off to do your offerings of rice to the spirits?" And he said, "Well, you know you taught us about Lucifer, about Satan, and how he is God's enemy, and how he's a deceiver, and we saw how he deceived Adam and Eve. Well, we now know that he's deceived us, and now you guys have come and you've brought the truth, the true story about the true and living God, and that's who we're going to follow. So we're not going to put up with that other stuff anymore. We just want to get rid of it, and we want to follow the true God." And that was after three chapters of the Bible, and that was mind-blowing for us.

From there, it was just this commitment to want to hear, this hunger to hear more of God's story, and to understand more of what He was like. And as that happened, we eventually, after six months, got to the culmination of the story, the death, burial, and resurrection of Christ, which made sense to them, because they'd seen it in the sacrificial system of the Old Testament. All that foundational teaching made the Gospel so clear, and I don't know, it's sort of hard to put a number on how many came to Christ, but the vast majority did. And many who didn't at that time did shortly after, as it became clearer to them. I can remember some of the young kids, actually, who caught on so quickly, explaining to the old people the Gospel, so that they understood it correctly.

Kaikou talks about how God's Word has replaced their traditional beliefs as the guiding light in their lives:

As far as God's Word in the life of the church, the view is that it is the truth, and that it has final authority. So now, in the lives of the believers, we see a real change in things that were formerly huge problems in the community; things such as death, or if sickness happens or arguments in the community. Previously, all of those things created tensions, but now it is God's Word that guides us through those things, and we really see that God speaks to us through His Word. Our relationship with the Lord has come about through His Word. The things that directed our lives, and that we trusted in, we know that they are not worth trusting in at all. We realise that there is nothing else worth following or trusting in other than the Lord Himself, through His Word, and it is only through His Word that we have come to know God and what His Son has done for us. And it is also through His Word that we have come to understand the work of His Spirit in our lives.

Here's an example of the changes that God's Word can bring about in what was once a warlike people group:

Today, God's Word has gone into all areas of their lives, and has made many, many changes over time that at times, honestly, maybe we didn't have the faith to see these kinds of changes. The people traditionally were really quite an arrogant people. They prided themselves on being some of the most fierce and ferocious warriors throughout that whole region, throughout that whole district. Some of the older men especially had been involved in some warfare. I remember sitting down with them in recent years and seeing a true humility that can only come about through God changing their lives.

THE AUTHORITY OF GOD'S WORD

We asked Bill and Kelley to reflect on what has changed in terms of who people are looking to for their authority:

> Their main authority was basically their spirits, their clan spirits. So when the Gospel came, those clan spirits completely went away, and basically what it left was a vacuum. Because at that point, when they first heard the Gospel, they didn't have elders. They had me (Bill) kind of as their pastor, but in the community, they didn't really have anything set up where they could go to for authority as far as even court decisions and life decisions that they needed answers to. The Lord was really faithful, though. He started bringing some of the teachers, giving them wisdom to be able to help with the different things that they were seeing in their lives, like, "Okay, how do we do this now that we're believers?" Things like that. So the Lord really started giving insight to the teachers for them to be able to help work through some of those issues.
>
> The neat thing about it was that the authority began to be the Word of God. As the teachers began to understand the Word of God and be able to explain it in their context, then the people started respecting them. We had this one guy who's one of the church elders right now. And the Lord was just really giving him a lot of wisdom in how to deal with problems that were coming up in the village, and he just has a supernatural ability, really, to be able to look at a situation and think about Scriptures that address that situation. And I've been sitting with him before and listening to him walk through things, and it's almost like his knowledge has expanded well beyond what I've taught him, and I can tell that the Holy Spirit really has taught him, and he can really bring that to bear on some of the issues that he's dealing with.
>
> One of the things that we taught early on, and it's something really special to Kelley and I too, is the story there in Luke where Jesus heals the centurion and the centurion's son. It's interesting that Jesus, after he heals the centurion's son, said of him, "Man, I've not seen such great a faith in all Israel." What's so interesting about that is the reason that Jesus said it to him. It was because the man recognized authority and he realized that Jesus just had to say the word. And if He said the word, then the sickness would be gone. And in that same way, we watched the church grow into that ability to be able to not just believe, but also to have a deeper understanding of belief to where they can start obeying and being obedient to the authority of Christ Himself through the Scriptures.

The testimonies in this tutorial describe how the authority of the Holy Spirit using God's Word has radically changed people in communities and is taking them on to maturity as individuals and as groups and is changing them in profound ways. It's hard to imagine something more exciting and fulfilling than to be involved in God's work of church planting and sharing God's Word in these kinds of contexts.

? DISCUSSION POINTS

1. Reflect on the statement, "We can be both learners and teachers at the same time." Think specifically about what that might look like in a cross-cultural setting.

2. In your own words describe what you would say are some of the most important factors in the authority of God's Word being established in a new community.

9.6 The complete narrative

> ✓ **OBJECTIVES OF THIS TUTORIAL**
>
> This tutorial discusses the fourth question in the area of Word: 'Are they growing in their ability to correctly understand God's Word as His complete Narrative, with Jesus Christ as the heart of the story and its interpretive key?'

> Hebrews 1:1-3: Long ago God spoke many times and in many ways to our ancestors through the prophets. And now in these final days, he has spoken to us through his Son. God promised everything to the Son as an inheritance, and through the Son he created the universe. The Son radiates God's own glory and expresses the very character of God…

Last time

We looked at the third question from the WILD outline. We talked about some of the factors relating to the authority that God's Word is given by people in their lives and among communities of believers. In this tutorial we will discuss the fourth question in the WILD outline which is also in the area of Word.

Are they growing in their ability to correctly understand God's Word as His complete Narrative, with Jesus Christ as the heart of the story and its interpretive key?

Dave talks about how the church they worked with were equipped to interpret life through a foundational, narrative approach to teaching God's Word:

> We were so thankful for the privilege of teaching the people we worked among foundationally and chronologically through originally the Old Testament narratives but then getting into the New Testament and teaching them foundationally through the book of Romans and other New Testament books. I honestly believe that the average Christian in that people group has a better cohesive view of God's plan as it is outlined in Scripture than a lot of Christians in our home countries who really haven't been taught in that way. As they face questions within their own culture, they are able to apply God's Word to them in ways that we wouldn't really even be able to because we

understand their culture to a certain degree but they can go even deeper and deeper and deeper and they are viewing these various areas of their culture now from the perspective of a Biblical worldview instead of their former animistic worldview. They're identifying changes that need to be made. They're identifying ways that their life can be just centered around God and His Word.

Bill talks about how teaching through the Luke narrative helped to tie the Biblical themes together for the church:

> I guess one of the things that's been a little amazing to me is that, as we thought about the developmental resources that we taught them through, we tried to make sure that they had the major points of the New Testament down. But one of the things that was really important was the book of Luke. We did that the very last. The reason we did it last was because we had just gone through a bunch of the Epistles, and we realized that, although we maybe in own lives could say, "Hey, this is what this looks like," we had never really spent the time in letting them walk through the life of Christ and watch Him, see how He was going to react to life and was walking with God.
>
> As they went through the book of Luke, they took all those examples of how Jesus did things. We started hearing a lot of different ways in which they saw their own lives and how they can apply it to their lives. I think that it was really important to let them watch Jesus Himself walk through the book of Luke and watch Him deal with people that were angry with Him, deal with people that were lying to Him, trying to kill Him. All the things that He was saying to people just seemed to come alive to them. I think that was just good to help them start really internalizing the message that they'd been hearing.

Matt talks about how they used a foundational approach to teaching, but had to make adjustments for the specific situation:

> Our strategies or our focus is to teach our friends who are wanting to be taught or open to being taught in their homes, teaching foundationally from Creation to Christ. At this point due to their work schedule and lifestyle, we're able to teach three to four times a month in that situation. It takes us a considerable amount of time to work our way through the teaching with them. Because of the exposure to the Catholic Church and exposure to other churches in our area, they have an understanding of some of the content of the Scripture but they have no understanding of the meaning of that content.

> One of the things we did recently with this family is, in our first conversation together, we gave them a panoramic overview of where the story is going. We started in Creation and we very quickly, in one session, went through to Christ coming back into the future. That has really helped us with them to keep them on the storyline and where we're at when we're teaching the Bible, and help them relate with what they're hearing in the story, how that relates to when Jesus lived and when they are living and keep it straight on the storyline, in line with history.

Philip describes a foundational, narrative approach to teaching God's Word:

> In the past, we had no understanding at all of the truth of God's Word or anything about Him. We had heard fragments of God's Word previously but it wasn't really clear to us at all. The way we came to understand the truth and come to faith was from hearing God's Word from the beginning. As we heard God's story, we understood who He is, how He saw us and the way of salvation that He has provided. Those who are teaching us didn't jump ahead in the story, so God's Word prepared us for the coming of the Saviour. And when we came to know Him through the story, our hearts were ready to accept Him as our Saviour.

Has their initial engagement with Truth introduced them to God as Creator and Lord, to Satan as Enemy, to humanity as God's lost race of image-bearers, and to Jesus Christ as Saviour?

We asked John, "What was the result of your foundational teaching approach?"

> Well, the result was amazing, and we saw the result actually happen back in the Old Testament. We saw, even as we were going through the Old Testament, that the people's trust was in this promised Redeemer. We hadn't told them about Jesus at that stage. All they knew of Him was that He was the One God had promised would come and get us out of this mess that we're in. And so, they had seen the Old Testament prophecies about the Messiah. And so, once we got into the life of Christ, we said to them, "Now if this Jesus is truly the Messiah, if He's truly the One God has sent to get us out of this mess, then He's going to have to fulfil all these prophecies."
>
> We had them written up and even though they were all illiterate, we would every so often read through this list. We'd say, "Now, remember, Jesus has got to fulfil all these prophecies if He is truly the One that God has sent." And so, as they saw the life of Christ and they saw those prophecies fulfilled, they became more and more convinced that He was the One that God had sent to

redeem us. And it was just amazing to see the things that happened.

Phil understood that the people there needed to grapple with the exclusive claims of Jesus Christ:

> It's been, say, five years since we've taught the first group with initial evangelistic teaching, where we started having believers. We've always felt like the challenge is it's easy to say, "I believe that." The question that we ask or that we wonder as they say that is, "Yeah, is that all you believe?" It's one thing to say, "I believe that and I've added that in with a bunch of other stuff I believe." So for someone to say to you, "I believe," if you just take that at face value and think, "Oh yeah they must be believers now since they say they believe this,"— it's not that straight forward.

Do they understand the Biblical Narrative primarily as God's interactions with real people, living in real times and places?

The believers in a Siberian community could relate to the struggles of the early church in Acts:

> When they were beginning, after we had gone through several foundational teachings, we began the idea of teaching through the book of Acts. As we were going through it in each individual group, what's actually amazing was that the different group leaders wanted to follow those patterns. They actually saw the persecution that happened around the church in Acts and the way that the families and the way the individuals didn't care for their identity in Christ, and they began to relate to that very strongly and they felt like this was a very real picture of what the church not only looked like for them, but what they thought it looked like everywhere in the world. It was their perspective of how the church is and they began to use that as a model which they would use to develop their own format of how they functioned as a church.

Philip talks about the central role that God's Word has in their community:

> In terms of the central place that God's Word now has in our lives, it relates to us coming to really understand the truth and the plan that God has for us. We have God's Word applied to specifics of how we used to think and how God wants us to live now. Now when death happens, or when potential tensions arise in the church, or if we have opposition coming from outside, we know that the only solutions are in God's Word. That's where both our defence and comfort can be drawn from because God's Word explains to us how Christ's work has completely changed everything in this new life we have.

Are they being helped to move progressively into new areas of God's Truth so that it ties in historically and thematically with what they've already understood?

Bill talks about the need for a teaching strategy that provides a church with a cohesive, Biblical theology:

> I think that one of the key things is to have a strategy to actually get yourself there. People don't just naturally come to an understanding of something unless there is a plan to actually move them from not understanding it to then understanding it. I think early on as we saw people—our teachers—develop, we started out helping them understand how to present things. And then once they got good at presenting things then we worked with them on how to actually add illustrations in, and then add application in. Over a period of time, as they grew in their ability to be able to present information and then to teach it, it started coming more from the heart.
>
> The last stage was actually leaving out a lot of the teacher's helps in the lessons and forcing them then to actually think through why they were saying what they were saying. It was that reflection I believe, as they were teaching the Word of God and reflecting and as the Holy Spirit was giving them insights, then they started seeing all the connections between the different things that they had learned and studied. Again, I just think it's important that you have a planned strategy to get there and not just assume that they're going to come to that point but actually help develop them to get to that point.

Phil describes how the ongoing teaching continues to reinforce the centrality of Christ in God's Word and in our lives:

> The thing that we're looking for and shooting for is the centrality of Christ becoming more and more integral and becoming more and more all-encompassing and all satisfactory for whatever problem might be out there, that He is the answer to all of that and there isn't any other answer. So as we see it, we want Him occupying more and more of the horizon of how they view life in general. They started out with Him there in the scene but he was inconsequential. "Yeah, we know that prophet's name. We know He's great. We know there's things said about Him in the Quran, yeah, yeah, yeah." But relatively speaking completely a zero.
>
> Through the teaching and through the lessons… I mean you're getting into Ephesians. There is no other power. He's ruling everything. You're seeing Him

constantly occupying more of this horizon of how they view life. And so that for us, as we see that growth, and we see these Scriptures that are communicating that, we're sensing, "Okay we're on the right track in terms of growing the centrality of Christ and the all-encompassing-ness of Christ in their minds and hearts."

We close this tutorial with a reminder of the importance of reinforcing the centrality of Christ in God's Word and in our lives which is found in Colossians 1:17-18. "And He is before all things and in him all things hold together and He is the head of the body, the church. He's the beginning of the firstborn from the dead, that in everything he might be preeminent."

? DISCUSSION POINTS

1. As you watch the tutorial video, note any benefits mentioned of a narrative or foundational approach to teaching God's Word.

2. One of the church planters interviewed said that many believers in the people group he worked with have a more cohesive view of God's Word than the average Western believer. Do you think that is really possible in a first-generation church planting context? Please give your reasons.

3. What do you consider to be the key principles of Foundational Bible Teaching?

➡ ACTIVITIES

1. Research and in a short paragraph describe Latin American Folk Catholicism. Note down your sources of information. What do you think might be some of the inherent obstacles, in that particular context, to a clear understanding of who Jesus Christ is, as the Biblical narrative reveals him?

9.7 Making use of God's word

> ✓ **OBJECTIVES OF THIS TUTORIAL**
>
> This tutorial discusses the fifth question in the area of Word: 'Are they increasingly able to make use of God's Word as He intends for His children and His Church?'

> 2 Timothy 3:16–17: All Scripture is inspired by God and is useful to teach us what is true and to make us realize what is wrong in our lives. It corrects us when we are wrong and teaches us to do what is right. God uses it to prepare and equip his people to do every good work.

That verse ties into what we're talking about in this tutorial. In particular verse 17 says that God uses Scripture to prepare and equip His people to do every good work. It highlights just how important it is to be able to give and provide God's Word in the hands of the people.

It's very easy for us to appreciate that in our own lives. Scripture helps us and teaches us and points things out in our own lives that we need to correct. So many of the strategies that are out there for reaching people just have to do with presenting the Gospel. But not a lot of effort is given to what follows that, what happens after people get saved. We see here very clearly that God intends for this people to be able to have His Word so that He can equip them to do every good work. That's necessary in order for that to happen. They have to have it in their own hands so that it can speak to their hearts.

Last time

We looked at the fourth question from the WILD outline. We discussed how people can grow in their level of understanding of God's Word as one Story, or Narrative, with Jesus Christ at the center. In this tutorial we will discuss the fifth and last question in the WILD outline in the area of Word.

Are they increasingly able to make use of God's Word as He intends for His children and His Church?

We asked Clark how having God's Word available has helped the believers there to feed themselves, to do correction and to reach out:

> I would say, because having the translations is fairly recent, we're just starting to see that happening. My example is going to be mainly with First Corinthians. We really consolidated as we were going through it, actually beginning to address areas of sin in the body. That became very important to them, which prior to that, they would just ignore it and let it go. They became very conscious of their responsibility to deal with it and how to deal with it and go in to one another. We've actually seen that the Word is what they'll take with them when they are doing outreaches. We've seen them actually relying more on the Scriptures than the lessons that they have. That's been a huge help even in the outreach that they're doing.

Are they learning to use God's Word to spiritually feed themselves and any others He has entrusted to their care?

In this next clip we hear how the believers in a church community are finding God's Word sufficient for all areas:

> Once we knew God, and that we were under His protection, we found joy in our lives and real peace. When difficult issues arrive in the community, the believers gladly come to the leaders in the church because they know that the real help lies in God's Word. They are happy to come because they know that from God's Word they will receive encouragement. They know that regardless of what happens, God has dealt with the major issue of the sin debt. They are always glad to be reminded of those things from God's Word.

Matt describes the importance of the church and community having access to good, Biblical resources:

> When we left a number of years ago, we had to leave for a pretty good amount of time. We left a lot of written materials, a lot of Bible lessons, a lot of materials in the hands of folks who aren't saved. As we're teaching, it's really exciting to hear their growing understanding of what they've read as they've read ahead of what we're teaching. A lot of the questions and a lot of the conversations are broader than just the actual lesson that we're teaching at that time.

We asked Kelley to give us an example of how real access (including literacy skills) to God's Word has served to equip them for using it in that setting:

> It is supernatural to see the Holy Spirit working alone. He doesn't work in a vacuum either. He uses His own Word and things of the world and helps them to apply those things. The literacy in our situation…they are untaught, uneducated, no written language. That took time, just putting time and principles and things into place that could improve that. And it took spending time with them: day in and day out doing Bible studies, teaching them to read, teaching them to read faster. It's very time consuming but they practiced it and spent all that time in the Word. That's where applications are coming from. Not only are they supernaturally one with the Spirit now, but also are spending a lot of time in the Word of God. The things that are being said, the things that are being applied, are coming straight out of that time spent. People are understanding Scripture and it's just flowing out of them.
>
> We had a lady who is now a lady's Bible teacher. There were some things that were coming up with some of the young girls. Her response to that was to have a Bible study. She got them together and we hadn't even translated the book of Proverbs, but just individual verses, and she felt like that was something that she could do. She had been reading it in the national language. She wanted to impart that wisdom to them. She started on her own, translating five to seven verses each week. Coming up, getting them checked, and leading the Bible study. Going through those we saw a drastic improvement in the girls. I feel like she probably carved off a lot of problems that would've come up later just by her ability to go and see a problem and want to fix it with the Word of God.

Palava talks about how specific teaching from the book of James about controlling the tongue has helped her:

> I wanted to talk about the effect it has on us when we hear teaching for the first time from the apostles. We see that it has a real impact on our day to day lives and we are grateful for that. We are grateful that as we are hearing it, we see the relevance to life in the community and it has brought real change. God's Word provides us with help in every area. That is something we really praise Him for. For example, I've been hugely helped by hearing the teaching from James that describes the right way to live together. For example, it discusses gossip and the harm it can do. It talks about this one small part of us, our tongues, that can do so much enormous damage. I am grateful to the Lord for the guidance He gives and how we should speak to each other. I have

really been helped by the exhortations not to be going around talking about people or gossiping. I am very grateful for that.

Are they using Truth practically to correct wrong thinking and habits of life, not in a way that produces fear and bondage, but real joy and freedom in Christ?

Dave describes how for the believers there, it was a natural thing to intertwine the Truth with their daily lives:

> Once they became saved, we continued with the regular public teaching meetings. We weren't teaching five and six days a week like we were initially. Still, we would have regular teaching meetings generally at least two days per week and they would come in from their gardens and everyone would be there. Along with the public teaching meetings, we wanted to continue to spend time with them in their daily lives as different things came up, as they faced various questions in life. We wanted to help them work through those and know how to apply God's Word to everyday life. Honestly, there were some ways that it's perhaps easier for them than it is for us in our culture because we tend to make more of a strict dichotomy between the spiritual elements of our lives and the everyday physical or just the common daily elements of our lives such as work and family. There are a lot of people in our culture for whom there are times where they're just really focused on their work or other aspects of just living in their home. Then they redirect their focus and now they're more specifically focused on God and their spiritual lives.
>
> Historically, they never separated the spiritual realm from the physical. In some ways, it was almost more natural for them to just keep the spiritual elements of Biblical truth intertwined with just the normal affairs of their daily lives.

Palava talks about how the things of heaven are more important than the things of the earth:

> Something else that has been very helpful from James is how we view possession. God's Word has explained that those things are of very little value and not something that we should be preoccupied with. It has put into perspective the things that really matter. Now when I go to town and I see things, I remember what God's Word has to say about possessions. It says that these things decay and get destroyed by rats and we know that we are going to be astonished by the things that God has promised in His Word. We are eagerly awaiting that.

Are they learning to reach out with the Good News of Jesus Christ so it is communicated clearly and faithfully within the Biblical Narrative?

Palava talks about the work of her and her husband, Kaikou, who is a teacher and elder in the churches in their village:

> In reference to God's work, I have realized over the years that it really is the priority over the other things that we might be involved in. This plays out in my role of working alongside my husband Kaikou in God's work. Sometimes it is difficult. I'm glad to do it because I know that the work I support him in is very important. I really respect him for what God has given him to do. He also involves me in it. I try not to complain because we are in it together. It is something we are grateful for. Even when it takes up a lot of his time, I don't resent it because it is God's work. I am fully supportive of his role in leading in the church and teaching God's Word. Often when there are invitations from other churches for help, he doesn't just go on his own. We go together as much as possible. We regularly go to churches or conferences for example and we see that there are often real needs we can help with there.

> We typically work with the leaders of the church and I will spend time with their wives discussing their part in the work. We also help local believers who are involved in translation projects in their languages. I talked with their wives about how as women we can be appropriately involved in the work as well. I am able to share from my own experience as being a part of God's work because I understand the realities of having a family to raise but also wanting to contribute to God's work. We can trust in God in these things because our lives are connected to Christ right now. We talk about how they can work in partnership with any foreigners who came to plant the church initially. My role is to help the women consider these things and have an effective role working alongside their husband and others.

When Palava works in the churches with the women, she considers what foundational truth they have available to them:

> When we are visiting churches in other language groups, often the women ask me some very in-depth questions. In that situation I'm careful to answer only considering what they have heard of God's Word so far in their teaching program. I say to them, I'm only going to explain up to what you have heard. That might be the book of Romans or Ephesians or whatever. I'm not going to jump ahead because those teachings, God's Word, and those areas of truth haven't been shared yet. It is their job to teach God's Word in the initial instance. That's not my job. I'm not going to take on the role of teaching new

truth. I just relate according to what they have heard so far. I'm not going to jump ahead because I respect the role of those who have come and planted the church there. I consistently don't answer questions if God's Word hasn't been taught and applied in those areas yet.

It's obvious that God has given Palava wisdom as she's thinking about the situations and opportunities that God is putting her and her husband in and is able to look at spiritual needs and assess them. In each of the testimonies above, it's obvious that God has given each person wisdom to be able to teach and bring His Word to bare on current realities. They were not just randomly following a program, but actually considering the spiritual diet that is necessary in order to move others on to the next level of growth.

 DISCUSSION POINTS

1. Try to imagine how your daily life would be different if there wasn't a clear translation of the Bible in your 'heart' language.

2. At this time, can you picture yourself being able to make the long-term commitments needed for equipping believers and a church in the way described by the people in the tutorial? Share any thoughts you care to as you reflect on this.

3. In the video a perspective was shared that literacy was a key factor in the growth of the church there. How do you rate the importance of literacy-based strategies in church planting? Research how 'orality strategies' have developed in missions and share your perspective.

9.8 Understanding true identity

 OBJECTIVES OF THIS TUTORIAL

This tutorial introduces the area of Identity, and discusses the first question in that area: 'Are they increasingly clear about - and able to articulate - their true identity from God's perspective?'

1 Peter 2:9-10: But you are not like that, for you are a chosen people. You are royal priests, a holy nation, God's very own possession. As a result, you can show others the goodness of God, for he called you out of the darkness into his wonderful light. Once you had no identity as a people; now you are God's people.

God created Adam in His own image. We see in this verse the idea of being image bearers, like Adam. And that's also God's intent for us, that we would bear the image of Christ, and that He would be our all in all; that He would be our identity. It says that we were not a people before we knew Him, but now He has made us His own people, His own family. Once we had no identity; we weren't anyone. But now because of Him, we are someone. Our identity as God's people is not because of ourselves but because of Him.

Last time

We looked at the fifth question from the WILD outline—the last in the area relating to God's Word. You'll remember it related to how people use God's Word to feed themselves spiritually, to correct wrong thinking and to reach out to others. In this tutorial we will discuss the first question in the WILD outline in the area of Identity.

Are they increasingly clear about - and able to articulate - their true identity from God's perspective?

Phil explains the two main factors in the people group's sense of traditional identity: Islam and the Clan.

> In my mind, identity had to do with Islam, being Muslim. That's what distinguished them from the neighbouring people groups. And so when they would trace their identity, they would be looking back towards the Arabs that came down and colonised this area a thousand years ago. There were Arabs coming here to trade before the Arabs were Muslim.

Being the last people group that's Muslim means they're surrounded by non-Muslim people groups. Islam, for them, is a huge part of their identity. I think it was Rick Love who has, in one of his books, this matrix: high identity/high practise, high identity/low practise, low identity/low practise. So, these guys are definitely high identity/low practise. That would be one of the things I would say that makes up their identity as a corporate people group. What separates them from somebody else is generally based on being Muslim.

The other primary thing after that is what clan line you belong to. That's where you get your prestige from, and that's where you get your sense of in-group belongingness from, depending on which clan you belong to. The clan then separates you by specifying who's in, who's out, who's related, who's not related, who's part of our joking clan relationship, who's not part of our joking clan relationship. It prescribes how you call people, what you call them, who you call them, the titles that you use, and the relationships that you can have with people. It's all based on your clan. I would say that's probably the two highest factors in identity.

Phil describes how the church planting team, coming from outside, were careful to distance themselves from unhelpful labels and forms of identity:

Right from day one, we came in and said, "We're here to teach you God's Word," while trying to separate ourselves from a particular identity like a church. In their case, they wanted to know, "Which church do you belong to?" And what was a relief to them was for us to say, "We're here not in the name of somebody in particular, like some particular group." For us, it's a distinction. Maybe it's a fairly fine distinction, but we would say, "Because we don't belong to one particular group, we're not sent by a denomination to build the kingdom of that denomination. I'm not here obligated to plant Baptist churches or plant Methodist churches, or plant whatever type of churches. I'm here to build God's kingdom, and that's my primary goal."

In that sense, it's like we came saying, "We're not here to build a church. We're not here to paint the name on it that says, 'This is the church of such-and-such a group, and everybody needs to leave their other groups and join this group, because this group is the only one that has the truth.' We're here to sit under a tree. It's for everybody. It's for Muslims, it's for Catholics, it's for whoever. We're here for absolutely everybody." And so we displayed that type of openness in terms of identity of who we were, and they're like, "Well, c'mon, you've got a group. You've got a group." And we're like, "You know what? We do have a group; being part of a group is something that human beings do. But we're not here to bring you that group. We're here to talk to you about who God is." And so, even though we belong to a group…I have a home church that's of one denomination, my wife belongs to a church that's a different denomination and our church planting partners are part of a church that's a totally different denomination. So we're saying to these guys, "We belong to different groups, but you're never going to hear us say the name of our group, because that's not what we're here for."

Phil explains that the church planting team positioned themselves as religious teachers in the community by the way they described themselves and lived:

In terms of our personal identity and how we presented ourselves to people, we tried hard to, again, not be associated with any particular group. We tried hard to work like this, "We're here because we follow God. We've heard His Word, we've understood it, and we sense this responsibility to tell other people what God says to all of us as His people." So as we were coming into this community, our own identity-building process is this gradual thing that takes place. First we're seen coming in with cars and generators, and we're put in a category of rich foreigner. What we're working towards is becoming known as people who, first of all, walk uprightly in terms of the local way of understanding walking uprightly and that we're people qualified to talk about our religious topics. We know about it, we have conversations about it constantly with people, and so there's a sense of authority that we know what we're talking about, and we can actually enter into these conversations.

Even in the Islamic side, for me personally, having read lots and lots of the history, you're driving down the road and you're turning to your Muslim guys and you're like, "Do you know who Hamsa was in relation to the prophet and how he worked with the prophet to protect him, and also to give him authority and to give him prestige? Because Hamsa, there was a supporter behind him." And they're like, "How do you know this stuff about Hamsa if you're not Muslim?"

And if there's a question about Catholicism, we're answering why things happen the way they do. So, by lots and lots of different conversations in the realm of religion, we're building the sense that we understand quite a bit of what God's Word says and what the history is, and how all these different religions tie together. So we're building this identity along the way of, I guess you'd call it, authority in religious topics, while trying to maintain a sense of independence about it without committing to one side or the other. If we're going to commit to anything, we're going to commit to who God is and what He says, and that's what we're trying to follow.

For instance, going to a mosque and praying says, "I'm here with you guys, you're my neighbours and I'm trying to understand how you guys live. I'm here to understand, to be a learner in this process." And so they're saying, "Well, you're not a Muslim." And I'll even, when I'm going in there, say to them, "Is it okay if I, as a non-Muslim, come into the mosque and sit and watch and see what's happening?" And then they wanted me to pray with them during that. They're like, "You need to come pray, too." And I'm thinking I don't want to create a scene here. So the question I asked them at that point was, "Is it okay for you if a non-Muslim prays?" There are people who believe that a non-Muslim's prayer voids the whole prayer for everybody. So I'm saying to them, "I don't mind praying, but are you guys okay with me being there? Because as a non-Muslim, I'll be voiding your efforts." And they're like, "Oh, no, don't worry about that." So there's things like that, where we're all trying to maintain a sense of independence and yet highly religious identity. That's what we were shooting for in that process as teachers.

Phil describes how they took on the community's identity markers to place themselves in the role of someone who could teach:

The identity that we set up for them right from day one when we first came is, "We're here to teach you God's Word. We're here to translate it into your language and teach you what it means, and what it says." So, their first introduction to us in the community was us putting ourselves in a religious teacher category. There's a lot of things that we're trying to do where we recognise young guys can get away with certain stuff, but guys in a religious teaching category in this culture need to act a certain way. They need to wear long pants, they need to typically have a beard. There're certain things that are associated, not that everybody does it, but that's associated with a certain role in the community, and we, to the extent that we can, match that role and those identity markers of that role.

Phil talks about how their refusal to align themselves to any religious identity has paved the way for the believers to do the same as they reach out to other local communities:

So there's that sense that came into it for us, to be able to sit down with these guys from the very beginning and say, "We're not here on one side or another side of this question. Are we Catholic? Are we Muslim? We're not Catholic, we're not Muslim. We're here to tell people about who God is." And so that sense of openness opened the door for us from the beginning and has continued to play an important role. When the guys are going to a new area, it's that feature that they highlight when they explain to people what it is we're here to do. We're here to talk about God and who He is. We're not here to build groups, we're not here to pitch one side against the other side. We're just here to talk about any group that there is.

And through the teaching process, the identity feature comes in even for me as a teacher. My team member, Francois, and I would often have this discussion where we're like, "It's not our job to wag our finger at them and say, 'You guys have the wrong truth, and you need to believe what we teach.'" If we were going to come down hard on one particular religion or another in a particular illustration, we would try to come down hard on all religions. Basically, we're trying to say, "We all have the same sickness. It's not you Catholics or you Muslims that are any worse off than anybody else. Here's what they do in my country that's not right. Here's what they do over here that's not right. We're here, we see you guys, we see things that are not right, but it's the same problem that all of us have and we're all, as God's children, as His people that He's created, in front of Him with the same issue."

And so, even in our own identity and in talking to the group, it wasn't, "Your group has bad doctrine. You need to take our group's doctrine." Instead it's, "We as human beings have this problem before God, all of us. My country, your country, we've all got the same problem. What's God saying to us that deals with it?" So it's that sense of us bringing ourselves in line with them and saying, "This is a problem that we collectively have as people." That identity we had I think was huge in the teaching. That was something that opened the teaching up for everybody, because it wasn't finger wagging.

Are they having their assumptions about who they are challenged and shaped by God's Word as it shows them who He is, how He sees needy human beings, and the implications of what Jesus accomplished on the Cross?

John worked with a group whose traditional taboos made them fearful of any connection with believers. They came to understand their true identity in Christ:

So, here we had a situation now where this group who were scared stiff of the church were now a part of the body of Christ themselves. And we explained that to them: that now, they were God's children. Now, everything was changed. And I think we went back over Phase One (the Bible message from Creation to Christ) again for them, the initial foundational teaching, just to really make sure that they understood it, and then we went back through that material, but from the perspective of them now being in Christ. This was to give them an understanding of their new identity, that now, no longer did they belong to Satan. They belonged to God. No longer were they shut out, but now they're shut in in Christ and safe in Him.

Clark explains how the people group's low esteem created obstacles to a correct understanding for the church:

> They were the bottom of the social structure in our area. They didn't have much of a tribal identity or an ethnic identity as a people, and I would refer to them as chameleons sometimes. They would blend into whatever community they were in, so they didn't have a strong identity as themselves.
>
> Again, they don't want to be singled out, so we find even as we go to town with them that they're not wanting to be identified with the foreigner as such. They don't want that scrutiny on them. They're very independent and individualistic. They don't play well with others, and they're happiest when they're in the jungle by themselves hunting or doing things like that. I don't know if that's speaking to identity, necessarily, but they didn't have much of an identity as a people group.
>
> They would find their identity in becoming Thai, or like the Thai nationals. So then you see Buddhism becoming a part of their identity that they're reaching for in order to be accepted in larger Thai society. That would've been some of the tension there that was going on when we moved in. I think as God's Word entered into their society, the main thrust in that was this desire to get ahead, to be better off. That was driving a lot of their initial movement towards God's Word. And I think now as we've gotten into Romans and some of the other epistles, they're starting to see that identity change to actually grasping and understanding that they're now God's children, and what that means to them.

Phil explains that even when someone is convinced of the truth, it is sometimes identity issues that keep them from faith.

> You'll get a lot of guys that say, "I hear what you're teaching. What you're teaching is true. What you're teaching is better than what I believe. It's truer than what I believe. I just can't believe it. I've got this or the other tie that keeps me from actually committing, even though I'm willing to acknowledge that in every way, what you're teaching is superior." And so, we're looking at that and going, there's something identity-wise for that person that's keeping him from it, even though all of his senses or all of his rationale tell him that

what we're teaching is better and truer. So what is that? And we're trying to look and talk as believers to say, "What is it that we can do? How is it that we can trust the Lord to tip the scale and get them over into the side where it's, "Why don't I just act on this and not just not act on it?"

Are they able to explain that they've been given a new life and identity in Christ, totally through the work of God's Spirit, and not through any inherent worthiness of their own?

Phil describes how faith in Jesus, in contrast to any religious system, has become a primary distinction of the believers' identity:

> So, where is this at with God? We're saying we trust Him, but in our back pocket, we've got kind of this backdoor openness kind of thing where we can get out of this, and we actually trust a few other things. And so, we're trying to work with them through this thing saying, "God's intent for us is total commitment and total rest in His sufficiency and what He's done on the cross." So we're seeing guys as they understand that, as they hear that, where in their conversations, their prayers, and their discussions and the teaching, there's this growing sense of, "We're people who trust only in what God did through Christ." And I think it was always there for a lot of those guys, that they really did only trust this and they realised this right from the beginning. As a corporate identity, they are saying, "And that's what distinguishes us from the people around us, because the people around us are trusting in what they've done. And we're trusting in what Christ has done for us. It's not what we bring to the table in terms of, 'Here, God, accept me for this reason.' We're coming empty-handed and saying, 'It's what Christ has done for us.'"

> And so, as that identity continues to grow and as people keep reinforcing, "This is what makes us distinct, this total dependence on what somebody else has done for us as opposed to what we've done for that person," that's what makes us distinct. Because there's a lot of people, such as the Catholics, who love Jesus and they're talking about Jesus and they've got crosses everywhere, and they don't have a problem with you talking about Jesus. But the guys are beginning to recognise, even though these guys over here talk about Jesus, what makes us distinct from them is that we're not trusting what we do; we're trusting what He did for us, and that exclusively. And that's what makes it clear, even for the Muslims, who are looking at us and wondering how are we different from the Catholics. Everybody's talking about Jesus. But what makes the believers distinct is that the Jesus that they're trusting is only Jesus. It's not the church, it's not the system, it's not the works, it's not

the Hail Marys. It's not the going to mass, it's not the being baptised. They're throwing Jesus in with all of that, whereas we're saying, "It's just Jesus, and what He's done."

Gebi talks about the fact that their identity in Christ is not just when they are gathered together but when they are in other places too:

> I am going to talk about when we go out to town and interact with those who don't know Christ. The thing that we are convinced about now is that even when we are out there, we are still connected to the body of Christ. Even though we are individuals, we have this clear picture that we are part of His body wherever we are, in town or wherever.

Are they realizing that although they are individual children of God, they are also a part of His family - a corporate identity defined by a shared relationship with Jesus Christ?

Greg talks about how an identity grew for the church in an already rejected subculture:

> When you're in a society like that for the deaf guys, there was no community. Their community was the deaf. As a deaf community, they united together. When they became believers, when there was a chance for them to understand God's Word, one of the ways we began is with just a foundational study together where we taught the Word of God together, where people sat around in a room where we discussed who God was, how God saw them, and then how God described the world around them. And so, as a process, they began to understand their responsibility and their need to begin reaching out to the world with this message of truth that had been given to them.
>
> So, as we gathered together in this group and they began to form this connection and identity of who they were, they realised there was a growing sense of them becoming believers, and they were being strongly rejected by the community around them. That began to help them understand and, in a way, to identify a little with who Jesus was and this idea of being rejected by men more and more. They began to form this close connection with each other that their life was seen through the body, that their hope was seen through each other, they were building relationships there. And then there was this desire to be able to reach out to the community around them.
>
> It was the same thing for the other people group we worked with when they began building relationships there. To be in that people group was to be Buddhist, and for them to come to Jesus Christ and to have an identity now in Christ meant they were seen by most of the community as rejecting the

Buddhist community. They're rejecting the entire community around them. And for many of them, even though they were from maybe wealthy families, maybe highly educated families, their families then denied them or rejected them and kicked them out.

For these people, because of the fact that their identity meant if you're a part of that people group, then you're a Buddhist. And for them to now come to Jesus Christ, that meant a massive upheaval in family. That meant a massive upheaval with friends, even with jobs and businesses. And for many of the believers, they had never expected that. They didn't understand it at first, but then they began to grow in the understanding of what that meant now to follow Jesus Christ. But the bond of the church became really strong, and the family became very strong, and this idea that we will provide, that we're the family.

We asked Dave, "What are the primary areas of identity originally and how has that changed since a church has been planted there?"

When we first moved in among the people, they had a strong sense of identity on various levels; the identity as a family, identity as a clan, identity as a village and identity as a language group in contrast with other language groups around them. There were serious obligations and expectations that went along with each of these identities. For example, if someone that you would call "brother" or would consider to be your "brother" asked you for something, it would be very, very difficult to say no. It's a little bit broader than the term "brother" for us. If they are in trouble, if they need help with something, you come to their aid, you stick up for them, sometimes even if it's pretty clear that they are in the wrong. You are going to side with these close relatives against the people that might be opposing them or accusing them, because that's what is expected.

The same thing happens on the village level. There were times where it's almost as if our village was kind of at war with one of the neighbouring villages. This was early on when we were still learning the language and culture, before a church was planted. And there was a strong sense of loyalty within this village against the other villages, and then when it came to other language groups, there was a lot of fear and suspicion when you would get outside of their own language group, to the point where they were pretty sure if you would venture very deep into these other language groups, you were very, very susceptible to being killed by sorcery.

> Well, it's been exciting to see these previous identities break down to where they understand right and wrong as the Bible establishes it, to where they would stand on the side of right, rather than just standing on the side of their "brother" or close relative. Also, as for these suspicions and fears that went into the other language groups, they found a oneness, a comradery, with many people in these other language groups because of Christ, because of their identity in Christ. At one time, there in our home village, we actually had a conference of believers, and there were people attending that conference from 10 different language groups. That would've been unheard of in the past. Many of the people with whom they now enjoy Christian fellowship are the children and grandchildren of the archenemies of their parents and grandparents.

Clark describes the journey for the believers toward a greater understanding of their identity in Christ:

> They grasped the idea of God the Creator. They have a very vague concept of an Owner, of a Creator, but it's very, very vague. So when we taught initially, that was what they grasped, that God was the Creator. He was all-powerful, then they would acknowledge Christ, but that wasn't who they talked about. For years, you heard about the Creator, the Owner. That was their emphasis that they talked about.
>
> But now and again, I think a lot of this has been because of the translation and stuff, and we've taught through Phase One and Phase Two several times, and we're starting to see that shift that now, they're starting to talk more and more about Jesus and His salvation, what He's done for them, and now being in Him. That's becoming more and more a focus of their conversation.

Phil explains that part of the believers' shared identity is their experience of God's Word and their complete dependence on Him:

> In their discussions with each other, one of the things that they call themselves is "the people of the trunk". We had used this illustration previously to say these are people who believe in the first three books and not in the Quran or the traditions of the church. These are guys that trust the Taurat, Zabur and Injil. So, they're calling themselves "people of the trunk" as one way of distinguishing themselves from other religious identities around.
>
> The other thing that they're constantly saying is, "We're the people who believe in what He's done for us, not what we do for Him." They see that identity growing and becoming stronger as they discuss it amongst themselves,

trying to differentiate, trying to wrap their heads around it. The negative side of what we've done, in terms of being un-associated with any one group or another, has been a sense of confusion about, "So what is it exactly?" Because people want a label to slap on it, to say, "This is what it is." So they've had to kind of develop and create this label, based on what we've been saying, what we've been emphasising. So when they're saying the believers' group, you'll see them stop from time to time and say, "What that means is this: we trust in what God's done for us. We're not trying to do stuff to earn and please God by our own efforts. We're trusting what He's done for us."

And so, "group of believers" is a fairly generic label, even in this community. But they're trying to work towards this identity thing of what they're saying. So, they call themselves the believers' group, but what does that mean? Then they add this qualifier to it. When I'm looking at the W.I.L.D questions, I'm looking at identity. The thing that we're looking for and shooting for is the centrality of Christ becoming more and more central and becoming more and more all-encompassing, and all-satisfactory for whatever problem might be out there; that He is the answer to all of that, and there isn't any other answer.

In this tutorial we saw that God's intention is for all believers to lose all other identities besides Him. All of us have competing identities. God is wanting to strip all of those other identities away from us so that our identity would be solely Him. Are we in Him or not? Because that's all there really is. There are just the two groups, and that's how we need to see it, and that's how those that we're discipling need to see it too.

As Christians, we need to be cautious of creating some other label for believers that would become the thing they rely on, whether it's a specific organization or some denomination, that would get in the way of a true understanding of who they are from God's perspective.

UNDERSTANDING TRUE IDENTITY

? DISCUSSION POINTS

1. What are some aspects of your own identity that you think could be; a) potential strengths, or b) potential challenges, to you being able to share God's Word effectively in a new community?

2. What are some aspects of your own identity that you think could be; a) potential strengths, or b) potential challenges, to you being able to share God's Word effectively in a new community?

3. Picture this scenario: After moving into a minority people group, you find there is a denominationally aligned church in a nearby town. It becomes clear that they exclusively use the national language Bible and are very tied to Western forms of worship. How do you think you might relate to this group, and how would you describe your relationship to them in the community?

→ ACTIVITIES

1. Research any churches in your home area that have a distinct ethnic or national identity. Find out what languages they use, denominations they represent, etc. Share your thoughts on the advantages or possible pitfalls of churches having ethnicity as part of their identity.

9.9 The narrative of the Church

OBJECTIVES OF THIS TUTORIAL

This tutorial continues to discuss the area of Identity, and looks at the second question in that area: 'Are they learning to see their story embedded in the larger Narrative of the Church, stretching back to Pentecost and forward to Christ's return?'

Acts 9:1-2: Meanwhile, Saul was uttering threats with every breath and was eager to kill the Lord's followers. So he went to the high priest. He requested letters addressed to the synagogues in Damascus, asking for their cooperation in the arrest of any followers of the Way he found there. He wanted to bring them—both men and women—back to Jerusalem in chains.

We're going to continue on with the whole area of identity. In the passage above, it refers to identity when it calls believers "the followers of the Way". These followers of Christ were facing persecution, and we see some of that in the narrative in Acts. The Church was just beginning and already it was facing trouble. We also see later on in the epistles that we're to be praying for those who are persecuted as though we're in chains with them. We are reminded over and over again that as believers we're part of this huge church, those who have since passed away and those who are yet to born. We're part of something greater. And it includes all of those who have been, are, and will be followers of the Way.

Last time

We looked at the first question from the WILD outline in the area of Identity. It dealt with the clarity of people's understanding about their true identity from God's perspective and if they are able to articulate that to others. In this tutorial we will discuss the second question in the WILD outline in the area of Identity.

Are they learning to see their story embedded in the larger narrative of the Church, stretching back to Pentecost and forward to Christ's return?

John describes how the church planting team helped the believers see themselves as part of a global fellowship:

> So here we had a situation there where this group, who was scared stiff of the church, were now a part of the body of Christ themselves. And we explained to them that now they were God's children, everything could change. And I think we went back over Phase One again for them, the initial foundational teaching, just to really make sure that they understood it. And then we went back through that material, but from the perspective of them now being in Christ. And this was to give them an understanding of their new identity, that now no longer did they belong to Satan, they belonged to God. No longer were they shut out, but now they're shut in—in Christ, and safe in Him.

We asked Phil how the new body of believers there were impacted by the teaching of the Acts narrative:

> I remember as we were going through Acts, and because of the way we did things we went through Acts pretty quickly and went straight from the ascension of Christ right into Acts. We kept going and were getting into the persecutions. And I remember one of the guys saying, basically, "That's going to be us. There are persecutions, people being killed ... that's going be us. Now that we believe like they do, we can expect the same response from the community at large, which is going to be people who reject us. The religious authorities are going to reject us."

> And I just thought it was interesting, not that we've had anything that actually has even reached a level of persecution, but the fact that they would recognise that would happen to those early believers. "Because we're in the same line as them, because we're in the same way of thinking as them, it's inevitable that we're going be included in those same types of situations." Even from the very beginning going through these ideas, I felt the beginning inklings of the sense of, "Now that we've associated with Christ in the same line, we can expect the same sort of treatment."

Is the shared experience of growing through the teaching of Jesus and His Apostles itself forming a part of their identity as a local body of His disciples?

Bill describes how being part of the Body, "Jesus Clan", didn't displace traditional clan identity but it has become more important in reality:

> I think one of the neat things early on before they were believers was they used to help all of their clan relatives in the gardens doing work. They would

all get together as clans and they'd work. It was interesting as we were going through Acts and understanding that whole aspect that there are actually just two clans as the Lord looks at it. He sees unbelievers and believers. As for the people in the community from different clans, I think there're about nine different clan groups. It's not like they left their clan, but they started seeing themselves more in this Jesus Clan than they were seeing themselves in all the other clans.

And so we would hear of work teams going out, and they would start cutting a garden. And where we live, it basically takes a bunch of people to get together to clear the ground, dig the ground up, plant everything. And we were hearing of these work teams going out, but the people that were normally in those work teams were different. It wasn't just clans anymore; it was believers starting to work together to do those things.

So that's one way that we saw them changing. I think another way was just this whole idea of, "When a problem came up, who was coming to help?" And one of the beauties of the Christian life really is that the Lord works through our hearts so that we learn to love each other. So when people had problems, there were other believers that were coming to them, helping them through situations. Before, people would just kind of watch things happen, especially if they didn't have any clan responsibilities. But believers started actually loving believers and helping each other out that way.

Philip explains that a distinction for them as a group of churches—in contrast to the religious groups—is their high value for God's Word:

> I will just add to what has been said about our sense of identity as a church. We see a real distinction between us and the religious groups around us. We are not trying to be separate, but we don't just go and join in with them for this reason. For us, God's Word has reality in our lives, in the life of the church. Actually, those who are outside see this is something that is distinctive of us as a group. So the centrality of God's Word in our lives has become an identifying factor for the true churches here, and that is exactly the thing that has brought opposition against us from outside. It is really the changes in our lives that God's Word has brought that initiated the antagonism of some in the wider community.

> The reality is that Christ's body does stand out as different from the rest of the world, and that creates tension sometimes. And part of our identity is that, though we are all individuals, we come together to hear God's Word, and to participate together in applying God's Word to real life. Then that can

be seen in the individual lives of believers. This sense of identity relating to God's Word is seen by the believers, but also by the unbelievers, and it has practical outcomes in the growth of the Christians and how they relate to the wider community.

Do they have access to teaching from the New Testament account that clearly shows how the truth given to the early Church also provides them with all the foundational truth for dealing with their own identity issues?

Phil comments on how important it was to share the life of Christ followed quickly by Acts, because it gave the people real-life, Biblical examples they could relate to:

> Going through the New Testament, in particular through the Gospels and into the early history of the Church, it was just so full of rich identity topics. Even when following the Building on Firm Foundations series, the topics or the stories that are covered in that series, which isn't very much in comparison to the whole set of Scripture, just in that narrow set there's already so much material that deals with identity. It deals with them, starting with Jesus and how He's interacting with a broader identity that's around Him, and how He keeps saying all of this stuff that says, "Now you guys are following a system." You can't fault the system per se—it's the Lord that gave the system back in the Old Testament.
>
> So they're following this God-given system, but He's constantly going after them because they've missed the point of the system. So you have religious leaders coming down on Him, rejecting Him, and He's constantly challenging them by saying, "No, you guys are the ones that have actually gone astray. You were getting after me, but you're the ones that have deviated from the true path that God intends." And that was extremely helpful for them, for these believers here, but to see this idea that here's Jesus fighting for this core truth that has been lost by the religious environment that He's in.
>
> So He fights for that, He dies in a sense for that. They kill Him, and yet at the same time there's this constant sense that, even there, the Lord's still parting straight down the centre line of what He intends, and how He wants to work. And then you have His followers coming in. They're afraid of the chief priest. What are they going to do? They're locking themselves in these rooms. They're afraid of what's going to happen. And then all of a sudden, they're coming out and they're taking it to the religious leaders. They're doing these things. The people love the story where the disciples were thrown into jail for speaking the name of Isa, and then the Sanhedrin meets and they're going to call them into court, and they send for them, and there's nobody in the jail.

They're right back there where you told them not to be, speaking those very same things that you said not to speak.

And for the amount of identity-rich material that's there, it's helping them to recognise that the broader system isn't and probably won't be conducive to us. It won't be helpful for us, it'll be just like those guys, and they've had to fight through the exact same things that we've had to. And I think that what was so powerful about it was they're saying, "We're not going through anything that hasn't already happened to those guys back there." We can look to the guys back in the early church and say, "They went through this same thing too." This is part and parcel, this is a normal thing, rejection by the authorities and having to formulate a separate identity out of something that you were a part of previously. And then there's certain aspects of it that you're going to reject, certain aspects of it that you're going to keep and discovering which ones to keep and knowing, "What do we keep doing, what do we not keep doing?" We've had lots of good discussions, lots of which have been prompted through going through the book of Acts, and looking at those different areas where it's like, "Well, look what those guys did. They had the same situation. What we're going through isn't unique in any way, shape or form."

Phil describes how the foundational teaching from Romans and Ephesians has helped to bring a sense of unity, even between former antagonists:

As a group of believers teaching them these days, we're in Romans and Ephesians, which we've done recently. And what strikes me in both of those books is how central the Jew-Gentile message is that Paul's bringing in both of those books. He's trying to take these groups that hate each other, that can't stand each other, that are at complete enmity with each other, that for whom the other group is just completely worthless, and he's bringing them together and trying to form them into this one group that's tied together by who Christ is. And it's been really helpful for us as we're going through that looking at identity, and we get these guys from these two different religious backgrounds.

And seeing them come together and seeing them hear that these guys hate each other, and here they are being brought together and being told to get along, and being told: "Even when your family is upset with you, why are you going and hanging out with those Gentiles? Why are you doing this if you're a Jew?" And if you're a Gentile you're like, "Why are you guys hanging out with those Jews and listening to all of this Jewish Scripture and stuff?" There was still this whole thing where everybody was blaming the Jews. They had to leave because there was so much tension.

So you're talking about these two groups. This wasn't some joke of a little flare-up here and there. They actually had to go. And so it's that sense that these guys who had such enmity with each other were brought together and joined together in one group with a different head and a different system of orientation. That must have just been incredible. So we're teaching through that and talking about that and highlighting that with these guys as we're trying to say, "This is what God's doing with you guys now.

Do they have a growing sense of who they are and why they exist as a group of God's children in that particular place, in ways that tie in with the Church's story, past, present and future?

Kelley talks about how the group they worked with in PNG were known as "the nothing people" but they now realize they have everything in Christ:

I think when you're talking about identity too, on the spiritual level their name means "The Nothing People". And it was really neat when we got to Ephesians and it says that once you were far away, and without hope. And as we translated it, it was, "You were wandering around thinking that nothing would ever come to you." We are The Nothing People, basically. So seeing their identity change from "We are The Nothing People" to, "We have everything in Christ," and seeing that shift from cargo cult into more of the spiritual side of, "We have these things later, we have these things built up in heaven, we have these things that will come to pass later." So on that side it was really neat seeing them pass from the have-nothings to the have-everythings.

Phil recalls how the story of Peter and John before the Sanhedrin inspired a young local Bible teacher facing opposition:

What happened was that, as this young guy was out there teaching, he was finished what would typically be in Phase One. He was going into what we would call the extended part. He was sharing through the Scripture at that stage, and he was in the early part of Acts. And two religious leaders came by that were big foreign religious leaders. They came into the area that he was working in. And they heard that there's a guy here talking about Isa. And they called a meeting and they said to him, "Tomorrow we're going to shut you down. We don't want you sharing any more about this Isa guy. We're going to shut you down." And he had a meeting scheduled that he was prepping for the next day.

So he goes home. He calls us. And he says, "Just so you know, these religious leaders came and threatened that tomorrow they're going to shut us down and kick us out because we're sharing about Isa." So we said, "Do you need somebody to come?" And he's like, "Just pray." Okay, so we're praying for tomorrow. So that evening he goes home, and he's prepping his lesson for the next day. And his lesson for the next day is Peter and John getting called before the Sanhedrin and being told not to talk about Isa anymore, and how they respond and say, "You judge what's best. Should we follow men, or should we follow what God says? For us, we're going to keep sharing. It doesn't matter what your religious leaders want."

So that's the lesson that he was preparing for that evening. And he's going like, "Ha! This isn't new. I'm in a flow. What I'm going through is not unique in any way, shape or form. The early believers went through the same thing, and they stood firm, and the Lord helped them and provided for them. So I'm going to stand firm too."

In the end, the local Muslim leaders, those two leaders that came in to put a stop to this for reasons that I won't get into here, they were chased out by the locals that night. So the next morning there was no meeting. Nothing came of it, because those two guys were chased away. But when that guy was talking about it afterwards he said, "What I realised then as I was preparing this lesson was that what happened thousands of years ago and what's happening to me is the same thing."

That last story shows how important it is for us to see ourselves as part of something that was founded at Pentecost. Hebrews 12:1-2 says, "Therefore since we are surrounded by so great a cloud of witnesses, let us lay aside every weight and sin which clings so close and let us run with endurance the race that is set before us." That's what that Bible teacher was doing; he set aside the sin and all the other things that were slowing him down. His motivation stemmed from seeing that there are others who have gone before him. Their witness is experienced today and shows that we're all part of this grand Narrative that God is unfolding.

THE NARRATIVE OF THE CHURCH

> **? DISCUSSION POINTS**
>
> **1.** A connection was made in the video between the shared stories or narratives of a group, and their identity. In your own words describe how you imagine the identity of a new group of believers could be impacted by hearing the Acts narrative together.
>
> **2.** Many new believers face opposition, ostracism and even persecution. If you were working in a situation where that was happening, how would you seek to bring them encouragement from God's Word?

9.10 One body in Christ

✓ OBJECTIVES OF THIS TUTORIAL

This tutorial continues to discuss the area of Identity, and looks at the third question in that area: 'Are they growing in their understanding of the bonds that unite them to the global/local Body under Christ as its Head?'

> Ephesians 4:4-6: For there is one body and one Spirit, just as you have been called to one glorious hope for the future. There is one Lord, one faith, one baptism, one God and Father of all, who is over all, in all, and living through all.

This verse reflects the reality of who we are in Christ and it's quite a stark contrast to the realities of what we're seeing in places where they have no light and are in darkness. It can be hard to understand darkness until you see people groups who have been separated from civilization. People often imagine these people to be some sort of utopian society where they're actually loving one another and they're helping each other out and working together in their gardens in the sunshine every day.

But we see in the case studies that it's not that way at all. These unreached people groups who are cut off from the Gospel and the light that it brings can actually be quite hateful towards one another and often lie and deceive one another to get their own way. In one particular story, we heard that the lack of trust between people caused them to live several hours apart from each other, even though they were in the same clan. But that's the heart of the enemy, he wants to divide, but as you see in the verses above, as believers we're actually united under Christ.

Last time
We looked at the second question from the WILD outline in the area of Identity. We talked about how people can see themselves as part of God's great Narrative, stretching back to Pentecost and forward to Christ's return. In this tutorial we will discuss the third question in the WILD outline in the area of Identity.

ONE BODY IN CHRIST

Are they growing in their understanding of the bonds that unite them to the global/local Body under Christ as its Head?

Dave describes how a common identity in Christ has broken down past tribal enmity:

> It's been exciting to see these previous identities break down to where they understand right and wrong as the Bible establishes it, to where they would stand on the side of right, rather than just standing on the side of their brother or close relative. Also, these suspicions and fears that that they had of language groups, they found a oneness, a comradery, with many people in these other language groups because of Christ, because of their identity in Christ.

> And at one time there in our home village, we actually had a conference of believers, and there were people attending that conference from ten different language groups, and that would have been unheard of in the past. And so many of the people, with whom they now enjoy Christian fellowship, are the children and grandchildren of the arch enemies of their parents and grandparents.

John describes how the church planting team used practical means to connect the believers to the wider body from the earliest days:

> We told them, actually, that it was their brothers and sisters back in Australia and America and New Zealand who had sent us to them, and all these other churches had played a part in them hearing the Gospel. And now they were part of this big fellowship of believers around the world because God's message had not only come to them there and to us in Australia and New Zealand and America, but it was also in other parts of Indonesia.

> And we told them about some of the people that had helped us build their houses, that these were guys who also had trusted in Christ. And so, on occasions if we went out to town, we would take them with us and we would meet up with other Christians and take them to church. Now, they couldn't understand church in Indonesian, but they knew that these people loved Jesus and that was important and they knew that there was a bond there, regardless of the fact that they had difficulty communicating.

We asked Bill and Kelley how the churches from the remote community in which they lived has integrated with others, including the majority culture church:

> I think one of the things that we did through the teaching, especially through Ephesians, was try to show them that we're all one in Christ. I think that

although they looked at us as being a different skin colour of course and a different nationality, they realised very quickly that we were one with them in Christ. It's been a little harder though with those in country as they look to the national church. For one, where we are located the national church isn't defined very well.

So they even have a little bit of trouble knowing what that is. Recently we've actually been living in one of the cities there close to where our tribal work is, and we've been able to kind of, not join a national church, but we basically go there every Sunday and sit there and just develop relationships. One of the things that we're trying to do is help that national church understand who this tribal group is.

Then when these guys come out we bring them and let them meet there too. So again, it's probably one of those things, it's a work in progress. We're seeing a lot of challenges, especially because the poverty levels and education levels are just huge. But we're just trying to help position them to where they're having to deal with who the church is and sort of ask those questions, and Lord willing, we'll see some growth in that area later.

In our context it's quite remote, so it's a six-hour canoe ride and then six hours by road, and so they're not really in contact with the national church in town very often. But they do know of other churches that have been planted in other areas nearby. We've been able to get them together and help them cross paths and do some conferences and get their relationships going and let them exchange numbers and things like that to try and put them in contact more and more with each other.

And it was real interesting, at the last conference that we did, on the last day we walked down through the village and there were tonnes of bags, these rice bags all piled up and we were like, "What are those? What are you guys doing?" And they had actually taken a collection. They had heard about one of the tribes that was there. They're much poorer. It's harder to get to. They're straight up on top of the mountain. They don't have coconuts, God forbid. And so, they were just really feeling sorry for these people who really didn't have a lot of material items.

And so they had gone through the village and they had collected pots and pans and a guitar and knives and clothes and they had all these bags, six huge rice bags full ready to go back with them. And so, I feel like they do, as they have contact, they do feel that identity, and as they meet they realise that there's other people out there that are part of this.

Are they allowing God's Word to define the proper basis of their relationships as a group, or do they seem to be unknowingly applying the values of the wider culture in the church context?

Phil describes how believers from a minority people group are learning to relate to brothers and sisters from other parts of Mozambique:

> We've had quite a few local pastors and local believers coming down to visit the believers here. They're always asking us, "Are these guys believers? How do we relate to these guys? Is this just somebody coming in for a visit or is this somebody that's actually one of our brothers or one of our sisters? How do we relate to these guys?" And so, it's been really good for these believers from outside coming to visit and for our believers to connect with them and to understand, "Okay, these guys are part of our family, and even though they belong to this, that or the other group, what unites us isn't that we're also a part of that group, except to say we're part of the group that follows Isa, and that's our primary identity."
>
> So, we don't care what denomination per se they're from or what religion, what is of interest to us is that they're following God. They trust Him. They know that He has to do everything to save them. It's not something they do themselves. There are other minority groups in which we're doing similar sorts of work nearby, and they're able to go over there and visit with those guys. If they have a conference then they'll invite believers from here. Now, we're careful which believers we'll send over there.
>
> I mean, it's totally a Christian area and when they go over there, the thing that they're going to do is they're going to slaughter pigs and that's going to be their main food the whole time. When we're sending people over there we know this is going to be a shock to their identity, even though they're growing and understanding and they're hearing from God's Word that it doesn't really matter. For someone who's still not used to that, to go into that environment and to be totally surrounded by Christianese and by pork and by all these sorts of things, for the guys here it's a steamrolling.
>
> We're careful who we send over there. We're trying to send people that we think can handle that, who aren't going to be like blown away and of weak faith and fall apart because they were eating pork at this meeting. And so, we try and be careful about that. And it's been good for them identity-wise to go, "Hey, we share the same belief, but these guys come from a totally different

angle to us." So that's been a good experience for those people who have gone and come back.

And what's important for them is this growing sense of identity because here they're a minority. Here they're freaks. Nobody knows what to do with them here. But one of the growing senses of identity is this connection outside. And so as they say, "You know what, there's a lot of other people that believe like we do, and when we see other people and we have this connection with other people and we hear what they're saying, we realise it's the same thing that we're hearing and that they're reading God's Word and we're reading God's Word and it's saying the same thing to us."

Then it's hugely relieving for them to have the sense of connection and it's encouraging to have the sense of connection. They are always wanting to send greetings to believers in other places and they're very excited to hear greetings from believers in other places.

Is there a sense that anything or anyone's authority to shape who they are as a church is legitimate if, and only if, it actively recognizes Christ as the true head of the Body? Whatever other factors might also draw them together, is it ultimately their shared faith, hope and identity in Christ that they see tying them together and defining them as a local church body?

Gebi describes how a common experience of God's grace has healed long-standing fractures in the community:

> In the past there were many, many divisions in our communities, and we now know that God's judgement was hanging over us then. But we were amazed to think that after hearing God's Word we became His children, as He brought us together then as one people. So as I said previously, we were a fractured community, as individuals, as villages, as families, as clans, but now we are one because of what God has done for us. So, that view of being divided has been replaced by a view of us as one in Christ.

> We see in John 17:21-23 the heart of Christ as He's praying for us who would come to know Him. And He's praying that we may all be one, "Just as you Father are in me, and I in you, they also may be in us so that the world may believe that You have sent me." He says it again, "The glory that you have given me I have given to them, that they may be one even as we are one. I in them, you in me, that they may be perfectly one. So that the world may know that You have sent me and love them even as You love me."

The testimonies in this tutorial are powerful. We saw that the testimony of Christ Himself is at stake, depending on whether or not local groups of believers would choose to see themselves as one in Christ and fight for that and prioritize that. And when that's done, then the name of Christ is clearly seen and God is honoring them and He's honoring His Son through them.

The testimonies are a powerful witness of Christ and His life and the unity with the Father. Within the body and within the church fracturing does exist. There is no utopia out there where people are just living in harmony. Division is something that is present in every culture, we know that. But when within the church—not to say it's ever perfect—but when those fracture lines that are always there in any society are overcome and believers do find that unity in Him, it shows the impact of God's Word.

? DISCUSSION POINTS

1. Describe some of the challenges that might exist for a new church in a minority group as it learns to relate to the broader national church.

2. In church planting terms, what are some of the advantages and disadvantages of a community having a strong corporate or collectivist culture (as opposed to a more individualistic culture)?

3. When someone comes into a community to teach God's Word, they are often given a specific religious identity and even labelled that way. Is that something you have thought about for yourself? Do you think you would avoid that kind of identity or embrace it? Why?

9.11 Viewing others according to the truth

✓ OBJECTIVES OF THIS TUTORIAL

This tutorial continues to discuss the area of Identity, and looks at the fourth question in that area: 'Are they learning to view others according to truth, and rejecting the divisions, biases and tensions that often define the wider society?'

> Galatians 3:27-28: And all who have been united with Christ in baptism have put on Christ, like putting on new clothes. There is no longer Jew or Gentile, slave or free, male and female. For you are all one in Christ Jesus.

With Christ as the center, you can see how divisions can be avoided. In the verses above, Paul is pointing out the past distinctions that everybody made; Jews not being connected with Gentiles and there being an animosity between one another, or slave and free or even male and female. Being united in Christ means that the divisions that used to exist are no longer there. So let's start living out what he's saying. There's just no end to the ways that we can differentiate ourselves from others but within the church, under God's headship, those things are eliminated.

Last time

we looked at the third question from the WILD outline in the area of Identity, which you might remember was about people understanding the bonds that unite them as part of the Body of Christ. In this tutorial we will discuss the fourth question in the WILD outline in the area of Identity.

Are they learning to view others according to truth, and rejecting the divisions, biases and tensions that often define the wider society?

Greg says that the believers were very tightly bound by intense opposition. Those early days were difficult, but today they miss the unity that came from being distinct in the society:

> One of the things that, for me, has been most impressive, and I've never seen it in the West before, was this unit that was so closely knit together by the body of Christ, the true sense of family, the true sense of understanding of

what that meant and the true sense of understanding of what persecution was for many of them and to watch them follow Christ in spite of those things. For many of these believers, today when we talk to them, they look back now and actually almost miss the days when they were feeling the persecution because of that unity that comes from persecution, that unity that comes from the world rejecting you and from being identified now as a believer in Jesus Christ. It was very significant to them.

Today, it's actually changed. In their area now, there are many churches and there are many believers. It's hard for them to know somebody that doesn't know a believer. Twenty years ago, they didn't know who Jesus was. Now almost everybody in the region has heard of Jesus and knows who He is. And that's changed the perspective of the church today.

Matt describes how history and current events have shaped identity there and the impact that has had on church planting:

Another challenging factor with this people group is they're reserved and very suspicious of outsiders. In the last ten or fifteen years, the illicit drug trade has become a dominant force in our area which has caused them to become very suspicious and very close to one another as well. And that has been really challenging for us as we've tried to reach as many people as possible, trying to pull them together to teach them God's Word. We found that they are unable to come together and so that's forced us into teaching in the small family groups. And that's slowing the work down considerably.

And even as a number of them have gotten saved and have trusted in Christ, this suspicion and the fear of their own people and of their neighbors is something they wrestle with and hinders them from really fellowshipping together and coming together to this point.

Matt explains more about the challenges to a clear understanding of identity and the impact on the small group of believers there:

When we start to consider these people and how they view themselves, and how God's building His church in their presence, a couple of things are really challenging for them. One is their view of themselves as God's children and their need to come to realize that, in Adam, they're separate from God. And they're not God's children because they're a particular people group, and that's a huge challenge in evangelism to see them submit to the Word of God when the Word of God says they're in Adam, and by being in Adam they're enemies of God. They're not children of God. They're not children of God;

that's the biggest hurdle initially for identity.

And then once they cross the hurdle, they join the body of Christ and because of the context of where they live, they join this body of Christ that is made up of Mexicans and them. And in their worldview, the Mexican is the child of Satan. And so for them to join a group that now has the ethos that we're all children of God because of Christ, means the one who was my enemy is now my brother. And so that's another huge hurdle that we see that they're having to face and one of the challenges of that is the believers are wrestling with whether or not to fellowship with other Christians because their people reject them for being affiliated with the Mexicans.

And so it even hinders their witness to their family because their family doesn't understand the Gospel, all they see is they're now affiliating with the Mexicans. So this concept of identity has got a lot of hurdles around it before they can understand their identity in Christ but also how they're connected to the Mexican population, the Mexican church, but also the fact that they're not Mexican and they haven't stopped being who they are by being connected to Christ. And how can they continue to be a witness to their family who now affiliate them with the Mexicans because they're no longer considered a part of their own people?

Are they increasingly less concerned about perceived differences with brothers and sisters from other cultural sub-groups, and learning to focus on the more fundamental common identity they have as members of Christ's body?

Kaikou describes how the strong clan ties that existed are being replaced among the believers by the ties they have in Christ:

> Within the church, there is recognition that a strong identification with the clan system brings division. Because in that system, everyone's efforts go towards helping the clan. But that has changed now because believers see themselves united through Christ's sacrifice and that they are one in Him. And now, there is a love between the believers that ties them together as one.

> So the help that they give to others is based on something different now. So now, God's children have learned to help each other, just out of true Christian love, and that draws them together. This has impacted the attitude of our local fellowships when they are planning for large gatherings. It isn't like it was before, with all the clan tensions. Now the believers generously contribute.

> We are very grateful to the Lord that we have seen this change in our fundamental attitude. And we want the basis for everything we do now to be that we are God's much-loved children. And because we see ourselves in Christ, we want to live our lives in the light of what He has done for us.

Gebi explains how God's Word has led them to put aside disputes and suspicions and traditional clan and family barriers:

> I'll just add to what has been said about the family and the picture that it provides. Before, there were a lot of divisions between families and also within families. Men regularly did not support their wives. And many would even go and live in other villages, away from them for periods of time and there was a great deal of suspicion between husbands and wives. But now, God's Word has taught us that He intends for there to be real companionship in marriage and that the family should be a picture of unity within the Church.
>
> In the past, the clan system created a real bondage for us. But now that we see ourselves as united by the blood of Christ, the clan system doesn't have the hold that it once did. We see ourselves primarily as the body of Christ.

Do they express respect and appreciation for the role of others within the church that is not based on factors like gender, age, education, social status, and wealth?

Clark describes how the church has wrestled with underlying suspicions and some negative aspects of relationships that were ingrained in the society:

> People began to believe and the church was born, but a lot of that suspicion was carried right over into the church. And you had family alliances and all of that was, it was pretty much a microcosm of the society. And then you bring into that the sons-in-law and the daughters-in-law, as they marry into families their loyalty is back to their original family. And the relationship between the mother-in-law and the daughter-in-law is just expected to be terrible. The mother-in-law treats the daughter-in-law as a slave.
>
> And we've seen those barriers both in the larger community but also within families start to break down. Just over the last year, with one of the families we're closest with, I've been in meetings where the mother-in-law will make a statement and be pretty dogmatic about it, and the daughter-in-law will speak up and contradict her mother-in-law and it's almost like lightning is going to strike. But the mother-in-law agreed, "Oh, yeah, that" and they were

both beginning to recognize the gifting of one another and being willing to submit to that. And actually for the mother-in-law to listen to the daughter-in-law, that's been amazing to watch. So it has those tensions, but you're starting to see them disappear. There's still some there but it's getting better.

Phil talks about how it is a healthy sign for a church when its composition reflects the larger society in terms of gender, age, religious background:

> One of the things that stuck out to me was when we're talking about that, we're talking about a body of believers whose demographics and whose representation and composition reflects the broader society. So that if you have a group whose composition is skewed, all men, all women, all this, all that, all one or all the other, and it doesn't reflect the society around them, that's something that you're going to say, "Hmm… I'd like to see that adjust and be a little bit closer to the actual composition of the community."
>
> So here, we're figuring it's something in the range of 95% Muslim and about five percent Catholic. It just so happens that the village that we're in happens to be one of those few villages that also has a Catholic church. A lot of villages don't, they just have mosques. So we have lots of mosques and a Catholic church.
>
> And so it's been really good, first of all we're teaching that we're not picking on any particular religion. It's kind of like we're picking on all religions in general. And so it's nice that there's this mixture so you can pull examples from both sides. One of the things that they constantly highlight is the fact that, "Look at us, we're people that didn't get along with each other, that always fought with each other, that didn't agree with different things. And now, here we are united because of who Christ is."

Phil refers to the variety of backgrounds among Jesus' disciples as an example for the identity of disciples in a church-planting situation:

> One of the things that we highlighted as we were going through the process was Simon the Zealot as one of Jesus' disciples and Matthew the tax collector. So here are Jesus and His set of disciples and He is inviting people from totally polar opposite ends of the spectrum. The zealots who are fighting, trying to get rid of the Romans and hate everything to do with the Romans, and Matthew who sold himself to the Romans and is a tax collector for the Romans. And so here the Lord is selecting from within His sets of disciples two people from absolutely polar ends of the Jewish spectrum and asking them now to unite.

And what is it that's uniting them? It's not some sort of agreement on this position or that position regarding what to do with the Romans. The thing that united them was now Christ is all. And that's what's pulling them actually together and being the uniting force in what otherwise would war with each other and not being able to stand the sight of each other. And so, we would talk about that with these guys and say, "You know that's what we're seeing. We're seeing people from a Muslim background, we're seeing people from different political parties, we're seeing men and women, we're seeing old and young, we're seeing rich and poor, we're seeing all these different guys. The thing that's pulling them together, that's the gravitational force that's at the center that's drawing all these different things in and holding these things that are in different orbits going in different directions. The thing that's the center in all of this is the gravitational pull of who Christ is. It means recognizing I can fellowship with you, not because I like your politics or not because I like your religion, but because you and I both are brothers and sisters in Christ's eyes."

And so we are seeing that rise up the ladder of hierarchy of identity. So you have this identity ladder, and there are certain rungs at the top that are high identity. And where people were at in relation to Isa was not a very high priority. So we're seeing people slowly moving this rung of Christ and who He is higher and higher and higher up the ladder of hierarchy until it's the top rung. And so that's been neat to see these guys being able to take certain rungs that aren't that important anymore and push them further down the ladder as less important because something else is rising in importance in their mind and that's been cool to see that taking place. We're encouraged by that. There's still a long way to go by far but you see movement and that encourages you.

Are they committed to reaching out to everyone, regardless of any ingrained prejudices in the society, so that people from all the different levels and sub-groups have access to God's Word and to the life of the church?

Phil points out that the teaching from the Epistles about the Jew/Gentile divide were truths that proved very relevant to the new church in Mozambique:

> As a group of believers, teaching them these days, we're in Romans and Ephesians, which we've done recently. And what strikes me in both of those books is how central the Jew-Gentile message is that Paul is bringing into

both of those books. He was trying to take these groups (that hate each other, that can't stand each other, that are at complete enmity with each other, and for whom the other group is just completely worthless) and he was bringing them together and trying to form them into this one group that's tied together by who Christ is.

And what's been really helpful for us as we're going through those books has been looking at identity. We get these guys from these two different religious backgrounds and seeing them come together and seeing them hear that these guys hate each other and here they are being brought together and being told to get along. They are being asked, "Even when your family is upset with you, why are you going and hanging out with those Gentiles, why are you doing this if you're a Jew? And if you're a Gentile then why are you guys hanging out with those Jews and listening to all those Jewish scriptures?" There was still this whole thing where everybody was blaming the Jews. Priscilla and Aquila had to leave because there was so much tension.

So you're talking about these guys, this wasn't some joke of, "Oh we had a little flare up here," they actually had to go. And so there's that sense of these guys with such enmity with each other being brought together and joining together in one group with a different head and a different system of orientation—that must have just been incredible. So as we're teaching through that and talking about that and highlighting that, we're trying to say, "This is what God's doing with you guys now." It might not be as severe as that separation, even some of the things that he says blow my mind, like where he talks about shaking the dust off your feet.

So if you're a Gentile, if you're a Jew and you're leaving Gentile territory and you're coming into the promised land, you're shaking the dust off of your feet because you don't want the contamination of the Gentile-ness to come into the promised land. So here's Jesus saying to these guys, "Shake the dust off your feet." It's like calling them Gentiles and it's like, "Whoa, you're calling us, people of Israel, Gentiles because of rejecting the Messiah?" That's pretty powerful stuff that highlights that with these guys and helps them recognize that identity formation is this huge thing that's taking place in Scripture. Everything from the story to the actual books that we're going through in terms of the epistles, it's just really amazing.

In this tutorial we saw that unity was a result of hearing God's Word. It's what allowed the churches to be able to reach out and to be a great testimony. Paul the Apostle wrote to the Romans and a big part of his intention was to bring unity under Christ.

When the divisions that are in the wider society are brought into the church, it is handicapped from the outset and unable to reach out. Church planters need to aim for a level of maturity that helps the church get past things that have kept them separated in the past and to allow themselves to be tied to each other through Christ.

We need to see areas in our lives that are contrary and the allegiances that we have that are keeping us separated. The Holy Spirit will use His Word to awaken us to see the divisions that are keeping us apart and the Lord will enable us to reach out, as it is critical for us to be united under the Head and to then be able to fulfil the function that He intends the Church to have.

 DISCUSSION POINTS

1. Research the situation in China where there is the Registered (Three-Self) Church, and the House church movement. Include a brief history, and whatever you can find out about the relationship that exists between them today. From your research, share any thoughts or observations you have related to the WILD question in this tutorial.

9.12 God's representatives

OBJECTIVES OF THIS TUTORIAL

This tutorial continues to discuss the area of Identity, and looks at the fifth question in that area: 'Are growing in their understanding of how to appropriately represent the Lord in their current spheres of contact and in others He might lead them to be involved in?'

> Romans 12:1: And so, dear brothers and sisters, I plead with you to give your bodies to God because of all he has done for you. Let them be a living and holy sacrifice—the kind he will find acceptable. This is truly the way to worship him.

This verse implies that we are to serve with our whole bodies, that we are actually part of the body of Christ with Christ Himself as the head. As servants of the church we're to give ourselves as a living sacrifice. After all, it was our Master who said, "I didn't come to be served; I came to serve," and then he washed the disciples' feet and told us to do the same for each other.

Last time

We looked at the fourth question from the WILD outline in the area of Identity. We discussed people's ability to view others according to Truth rather than based on pre-existing divisions, biases or tensions in the wider society. In this tutorial we will discuss the fifth question in the WILD outline in the area of Identity.

Are they growing in their understanding of how to appropriately represent the Lord in their current spheres of contact and in others He might lead them to be involved in?

Greg describes how the deaf are often marginalized in Siberian society but the church is finding fertile soil among them:

> One of the challenges for deaf people is, if you're deaf in Siberia, most likely you have been raised in an orphanage. That is where you have grown up in, that's all you have known all your life. And when you're out of the orphanage at the age of 21, you're on the street. So most of these guys don't have families, don't have connections, and so how do they survive where most of

the guys end up in crime? They end up in some kind of a system that actually provides for them, but also protects them in the society.

The church has actually found a way to become part of that connection. To become an avenue outside that life of crime. So they actually get involved with young kids in the schools. In these orphanages that they work in, they've provided jobs for people. They actually go in and they provide livelihood for guys. Actually through that they are discipling and mentoring people and are using that as a method to bring them into the body of Christ.

Are they wrestling with the practical realities of what it means to be relevant representatives of Christ in their particular contexts?

Kaikou describes how they as communities of believers see themselves in relationship to those who haven't yet come to faith:

> In terms of how we see ourselves, our sense of identity, we are very thankful to the Lord that we see major changes in our views. Our understanding of these things plays out when we are travelling. I am talking about when we go out of our traditional area and go to the market in town, for example, or go somewhere else to play sports. So it isn't like we want to separate ourselves from everyone.
>
> Because you can't live like that anyway. We all have to live out in communities and spend time with people who are not yet clear about the truth. Like I said, there has been a huge change in our view of things, and it is related to the life we have in Christ. Our view of these things has radically changed because we see other people involved in things that we previously thought were okay. But now, we don't want to involve ourselves in many things related to that former life. Our thinking has changed and it has to do with our identity. Because now we understand the way that God sees us. Being conscious of that makes us want to live as He wants us to.

Bill explains how the leaders of the young church had to wrestle with understanding their relationship to the community:

> One of the things that the elders of the church really struggled with early on was, as they started gaining wisdom in the Scriptures, all the people in the village started coming to them for counsel. They became a very huge burden for the elders because everybody in the community started bringing problems to them.
>
> So we had to sit down with the elders and help them determine what was a

community issue, and what was a church issue. The church issues we tried to keep those for the elders, and then the community issues we tried to let them be dealt with by the village leadership. Now of course when it became believer to believer the elders dealt with that, but there were some unbelievers in the village that were causing problems and the elders ended up trying to solve all that. That was something that we really had to help them work through, determining what was the church issue and what they should push over to the village leadership.

Matt explains the dilemma of young believers as they face being ostracized for their involvement with other believers:

"One of the challenges for the people in our area was that part of their identity involved participating in the cornbeer culture where they make beer out of corn and every event in life that's significant is encapsulated in a cornbeer party. It has to have it. And if you don't make cornbeer on the proper days, you're no longer considered one of the people. And the believers, on their own initiative, stop making cornbeer and stop going to parties, so their families basically say they are no longer part of the group for that and that hinders their ability to be a light and a witness to their families and so these are things we're wrestling with right now. We really are trusting God with this small group of believers to figure this out.

How can they continue to be a light to their families, continue to have opportunities with their families. We have practical conversations with young men who are believers, but who are wrestling with questions of, "If I identify with the church, I no longer have relationships with my cousins and my uncles who I want to reach with Christ, so how do I do that? Do I identify with the church and be rejected, or can I identify with them and then be rejected by the church, but now I'll be a light to my family?" These are the issues that the young believers are wrestling with today as we are working with them.

Is their growing understanding of being God's servants resulting in an expanding view of "the world" as He sees it, and the role they can play in providing access to the Gospel?

John recounts how, after hearing the good news, the people there were immediately burdened for their distant family members:

The young fellow who helped me put the lessons together was Habianna. The day we finished teaching on the ascension of Christ, he said to me, "I'm leaving. I've got to go and tell my mother this story." And I said, "Where's your mother?" And she was days walk away, but he was going to walk for days. And he said to me, "I just hope I can remember it all because it's a long story." But off he went. He immediately had this burden that others would also know this incredible story, that he had just finished hearing for the first time.

Bill describes how the churches in the isolated people group where they live have begun to consider their responsibility to reach out to other groups:

> Where we live, we're very isolated in the people group that we work with that is very isolated too. There are other language groups that border them, but they are pushed quite far away. And of course the language is different, which makes them really isolated from each other. There are multiple churches now in our language group, so that means that those churches border several of the language groups. There are always marriages that happen in between. We have really worked with the churches to try to position themselves in a way that they can actually do ministry. Although I don't think that we've seen a lot of growth in this area, it's something we continue to help them work through and kind of always pointing them towards the needs that are out there.
>
> Over these last couple years we have seen the church where we live look to the different language groups that are bordering them and start asking the question without us pressing them to start asking the question: "What's our responsibility in this and how can we be of help even if it's something small?" They are starting to ask the questions. So we're just hopeful now that as the questions are starting to be asked that the Holy Spirit will also start giving them ideas on how they can bridge that gap that's always been a deterrent for them.

God intends for us as believers to see ourselves in Christ and find security in that. If we are insecure in Christ, then we are unable then to reach out to others. And if we see ourselves in Christ, then it won't make a difference to us whether we are rejected or whether our message is received.

As we wrap up the topic of identity in this tutorial, we see just how crucial it is for us as individual believers. When we are secure in Christ, then we are actually able to be a light to the world. When we are not secure and are reaching out to other things to find satisfaction or to find our identity in, then they become idols to us, and our testimony is hindered. This is important for us to consider for ourselves, as we are wanting to see this in the people that we are reaching. We want them to grow in their understanding of the reality of who Christ is for them.

? DISCUSSION POINTS

1. Imagine a small church in what has traditionally been a marginalized minority group (maybe you know of or can research a situation like this). Thinking specifically of identity, what are some of the challenges a group of believers in that situation might face as they seek to reach out to the broader community/culture?

2. Do you agree that the initial identity and roles that a church planter takes on in a new context will have a direct effect on how the group of believers eventually come to see themselves in the community? Please explain your thoughts.

3. In terms of identity, what would you say are some of the factors in a group of believers accepting their responsibility of reaching out with the Gospel as part of the Body of Christ?

9.13 A relationship with Jesus

✓ OBJECTIVES OF THIS TUTORIAL

This tutorial looks at the first question in the area of Life: 'Are they experiencing a deepening relationship with Jesus, learning to depend more completely on Him in different areas of their lives, and gradually seeing their values and behavior change as a result?'

> Genesis 2:7: Then the Lord God formed the man from the dust of the ground. He breathed the breath of life into the man's nostrils, and the man became a living person.

It was through God breathing into Adam that he actually came alive. Previously he had the actual form of a man, but it wasn't until that process that he came alive. We'll be talking about the life that God intends for us to have in Him. The idea of the Holy Spirit actually comes from this Hebrew idea of breath. And apart from the Holy Spirit giving life and living through us, we're dead just like Adam was.

The Holy Spirit came in and dwelt in the church and gave the church life. Without Him, we're unable to perform the things that God intends. And even a local representation of the church can't do the things that God wants it to do, apart from His breath, apart from His quickening, to use that old term, through His life-giving Spirit.

Last time
We looked at the fifth question from the WILD outline in the area of Identity. It related to people's ability to appropriately represent Christ in their context and community. In this tutorial we will discuss the first question in the WILD outline in the area of Life.

Are they experiencing a deepening relationship with Jesus, learning to depend more completely on Him in different areas of their lives, and gradually seeing their values and behavior change as a result?

Kaikou explains how their lives and activities have changed as they have understood God's grace:

> As far as the topic of God's view of us as His much-loved children, we have come to understand God's great love for us and that has really impacted our thinking. Understanding God's love has impacted our lives in very real ways.

For example, in the rituals that were done at funerals, and the costumes that were done for firstborn children and initiation rites, and the songs and dances related to death and marriage. We have changed in all of that completely.

But now that our identity is in Christ, we sing about Him and His grace. So whether we are in our homes, or working in our gardens, or just around we are often singing about Him and our salvation.

We asked Bill what they looked for to indicate a deepening relationship with the Lord Jesus:

As we looked at the church we asked ourselves, "Okay, we're going to be doing all this teaching and they're going to have a lot of understanding, but at what point are we going to interact with them on that relationship that they have with the Lord?" And I think there were two things that really stood out to me that gave me encouragement. One was when you just asked them, "What are you reading? What are you studying?" you start hearing stories of, "Man I laid in my bed last night for hours reading and praying." And you start seeing the time that they're spending with the Lord and the interaction and just listening to their conversation, and you realize that they're not taking a test here; they're telling you how they're feeling.

But I think probably the biggest thing that opened my eyes to how they were relating to the Lord was to listen to them pray. One of the things, that of course we got from the Building on Firm Foundations series, was that when we prayed in front of them, we did not have these long eloquent prayers. They were very simple and to the point and yet after a while when you heard them pray, you're thinking, "Where in the world did they get this from?" Because they are very relational, their eyes are open, they're just talking and from their conversation you can tell that they're talking to Somebody, and you can definitely see the growth that they're having with the Lord as they start praying.

So that was one way. We actually documented that in their services, listening to them pray, what they were praying for. Early on it was more physical. As they grew and matured, those prayers suddenly stopped. There's still things in there about their physical lives, but they mainly started focusing on those identity issues, who they were and that they would remember that when they were tempted to sin and especially the hope that they had, one day being able to leave all this earthly pain and trouble and be with Christ forever. You started seeing that much more in their prayer. So, I think that was one way that we saw that it developed.

Kelley describes how the uncluttered lives and holistic view of the believers is a help to them:

> There's no doctor, it's a hike to the nearest house or the nearest aid post and there's not a lot of helps in any area of life. And so when they need something they're so quick to pray. And I remember one time walking down to our elder's house and I had heard that his daughter was sick with malaria. So I said, "Well, have you taken malaria medicine yet?" There's a place where one of the men has been trained to sell it. And he goes, "No, I haven't been down there yet. We haven't even prayed about this yet."
>
> But they're just so quick to call out to Him because there's no one else. And so quick to spend time with Him, because they don't have other things going on. So they're in the garden, and they're talking with the Lord, and they're on the trail. And they're talking to you, and then they're talking to God, and they're praising God. And so, just their lives are not dichotomized like ours, they live so holistically. They believed in the spirit world before. So this is not new to them. So they're actually the experts when it comes to prayer and spirit life. And we're the learners now because we've lived in a materialistic scientific world.
>
> But just to watch them and hear them pray and just the childlikeness of it and then hearing them talk about heaven! I tell people I'm embarrassed and humbled when I sit with the ladies and listen to them talk about heaven because it is so real for them and it is that rest they look forward to because they have no rest. They are still living in the middle of the curse, they are still sweating, they are still feeling the pain, they're still working the ground, and they're still having babies without any anesthetic. And so they are still right there in the middle of it and they long for heaven like I have never longed for it because we have so many comforts.
>
> And so just sitting with them is therapy about where the reality is and where we're going. How they're viewing it is always an encouragement to us to think and pray differently and more personally than we do.

Is their relationship with Jesus producing thankfulness, stability, authenticity, a willingness to serve others, and confidence about eternity?

Greg describes how God's Word has brought about love and acceptance between the believers as they live as a community of faith:

> Part of the whole picture as we've watched the church grow is that we've seen the church continue to have a real sense of their identity, where they

were at. They are beginning to understand who they were before Christ and now seeing who they are now in Christ, and we are seeing that develop into a life, into a community, and affecting how they function with one another, how they can help each other. We've watched the church grow in an understanding of who God is and how He sees them as people and how then they live out that life amongst themselves as a community and it has been a real pleasure to watch.

The Holy Spirit's impact on many lives has been unique in how He touches people and how He impacts them. They are deepening in their understanding of how God sees them, and how God loves them, what we see through Scripture, how the church should function as a body, how they should bless and encourage one another, how to help each other and how to actually engage with one another.

The church being family has been huge, where they actually see that together they're united, together they're stronger. They care deeply about the needs of each other, that the family is all there.

John remembers how the believers found freedom from old taboos and through music began to celebrate their life with Jesus:

One of the things that happened immediately after we had believers was we said to them, "Your brothers and sisters around the world, they talk to God." So we talked about prayer. And we told them, "and they sing to God, and they worship God and they tell Him how thankful they are for what He's done." And so they said, "Well, can you give us some of these songs so that we can sing them?" And we said to them, "Well look, God's put a new song in your heart. All the things you're feeling about Jesus, all the love you have towards Him, you can express that in a very special way through music."

Now that was another thing that the spirits had denied them. They believed that if they sang, the spirits would be angry. So they had nothing to do with music. And so now, this opened up a new area of music to them. And they would hear us playing songs on tape recorders. And so we said to them, "You start writing songs." Well I tell you what, some of these songs, the first song they ever put together, it went on forever. They tried to put the whole Bible I think in one song, but the theme was "only Jesus could do it". Only he could do it, no one else could save us, only He. There was this affection for Christ that was so obvious.

John goes on to describe how the believers' prayers were full of thankfulness:

They had no word in their language for "thank you". I'm sure they had ways of expressing it in their culture. And so we had to introduce the Indonesian word into their language. But their prayers were full of thankfulness for what God had done, that these people who they knew were considered by many to be half animal and half human, God loved them so much that He sent His Son to die for them. And that had a profound effect upon them. So we saw their thankfulness, we saw it in relationships; we saw changes in how men acted within the family especially in the responsibility that they began to take to help their wives. There were tangible signs.

I remember, I think the first day when we were moving around to the houses, just asking them about their response to what they'd heard and basically looking for testimony of whether or not they believed. What I heard, from almost all of them was, "Yes, absolutely. Christ is my Savior, He's my substitute. He's paid the price for my sin."

John describes how they saw significant changes in relationships among God's children:

If ever they heard of anyone in need, man, they were there like rockets. They just had that heart to care for people. And they knew that because God cared for them, they would show that same love and concern for others. So we did, we saw people becoming generous and caring for one another, giving to one another.

Before, that was all based on obligation. You could ask for anything from anyone and they had to give it, but then they knew very well that sooner or later, you'd be after something from them. Now there was a desire to just look out for one another because God looked out for us. He was the example of how we were to live, Jesus was the model and so there was a real concern for us praying for one another. We took a little girl out to town who had a gut obstruction and needed an operation. The whole group all got together and just prayed. There was this dependence on God in prayer.

Bill describes how believers learned to truly care for each other:

It wasn't just clans anymore; it was believers starting to work together to do those things. That's one way that we saw them changing. I think another way was just this whole idea of when a problem came up someone was coming to help. One of the beauties of the Christian life really is that the Lord works through our hearts so that we learn to love each other. And so, when people had problems, there were other believers that were coming to them helping them through situations where before people just watched things happen, especially if they didn't have any clan responsibilities. But believers started actually loving believers and helping each other out that way.

Are they able to identify old habits of dependency that get in the way of completely relying on Christ for their standing in God's eyes and for all their true needs?

Dave describes how the new believers gradually left behind religious and cultural practices that were at odds with truth:

> When the people first became believers, some of them were still holding on to some of the older traditional beliefs. There was a tremendous amount of pressure on them to still do some of these incantations, these rituals to make their food grow. Also, especially for the village leaders, the clan elders, there was a tremendous amount of pressure on them to do these cultural celebrations that really were mostly designed to raise their status to prove that they are a powerful, important leader in the village.

> Some of them did partly give in to some of these traditions but eventually we saw the believers come together and discuss these things. They said, "This really is not acceptable. These are old practices. It does not lift up the name of the Lord. It lifts up our names and it's turning our eyes away from God." And the people together were able to understand that and come to those conclusions. And it was exciting to see them do that.

> We didn't go out and just clobber them over the head for not maybe immediately dropping some of these cultural practices because we wanted it to be something that really came from their heart. We didn't want them to be conforming to our wishes as outsiders. So, we continued teaching them God's truth and it was exciting to see God's truth having effects in their lives, in areas that were very deep seeded culturally for generations among them, and yet they began to gradually let go of those.

> Of course they realized more fully what it meant to pray to God and that replaced these incantations. We needed to make sure they clearly understood that prayers are not just the incantations with just a slight twist, just a slight difference. And at first, perhaps some of them might not have fully understood that, but I think most of the believers really do.

Matt gives an illustration of how a relationship with God is helping a believer deal with fear of the spirits:

> We've seen, in a number of different ways and a number of different friends'

lives, how the Word of God is becoming an authority in their life and changing their whole lives. They are used to being fearful of the spirits, being fearful of the dead spirits or the dead ones or the ghosts. They live in constant fear of those spirits. And we've seen with those that have trust in Christ and have understood who He is, that He's their Creator, and that He is their Savior. And as they grow in that understanding based on the Word of God, their fear dissipates.

One of our friends, a very fearful lady, mother of nine or ten children, lived with fear every night. She would say she would hear the spirits of the graveyard. She lived next to an infant graveyard, and she would hear those spirits every night and hear babies crying and hear all kinds of things that would just capture her in fear. And then she grew in her understanding of who Christ was, and that He's in her life as a believer.

She told my wife that from one day to the next, she no longer heard those babies crying. She no longer lived in fear. And when her husband would leave to work and be gone for days on end, when she was overwhelmed with fear or felt fear coming in, she would just recognize in prayer and just say, "Lord you're here with me. Your Word says You are here with me. You're my Savior, you're my Creator." And all the fear would dissipate in her life and now she lives a bold life. How the Word of God just keeps shaping her is so exciting to watch.

Is the direction of their lives gradually changing, not through their own efforts to try to be "Christian," but as the Spirit teaches and equips them to live out the attitudes of Christ in valid ways?

Phil explains how they taught that God's intention is to live His life out through His children when they depend on Him and not their own efforts:

> That's the core element of the questions, "What is it for ministry? What is it for life, what is it for anything?" It's this relationship to the Lord that has this outer flow into so many other different areas, whether I'm communicating about that life or whatever it happens to be. But that is, in my mind, the core essential element. And so as we're communicating with these guys we're saying, "That's what God's looking for." His standard for whether or not you're one of His children is whether you have Him in you.
>
> How you have Him in you is because you accept the sin problem and accept His remedy for it. Then He gives you His Spirit to live inside of you. Now, you are the temple of God, not the temple made with human hands, but the temple that He made that He wants you to live in. And not just you individually,

but you corporately as a whole body. The temple is both individual human beings and the corporate body of Christ. And so He's working inside of you, and He's wanting this thing to flow into every area of your life. And He's wanting this relationship to be the source for everything and for Him to be the power for everything that's happening. So, whatever you're doing, He wants it to be something that's done through His power, through His leading, that He's telling you to do this. You're doing it in dependence on Him and that's the basis for everything that you're doing.

So there's constantly this attempt to confront and undermine the works mentality when somebody says, "I gained relationship by virtue of what I do." And so, we've told lots of stories about it in different analogies where we're trying to explain it to people. We're trying to help them understand. I guess one of the easiest ones probably to grasp it—and we've had this discussion with a lot of individuals around Ramadan that we just started yesterday or the day before—is the story of Cain coming to the Lord.

Cain, he's a gardener and he's taking the best of what he's got. The issue isn't that he's bringing food, it's that he's bringing something that he's done. So it's almost like this basket that he's bringing to the altar. And he's put in there the best that he can drum up. The choicest foods and everything like that, that he's bringing these offering to the Lord. God is like, "No, the principle's wrong. It's not how good this fruit is, it's something that you've created."

So, when we were doing this illustration many times over the teaching, we said that it's like I have this big basket and I put it on this altar and say, "Well Lord, I'm bringing this and I'm bringing this." When we got into speaking about salvation, it was the same thing. We took the same basket, "Well, I prayed five times a day, I got baptized, I fasted." It's like all these things that we've put in this basket are going to save us. As if it's things that we've done and things that are coming out of our own effort to earn something and we're hoping that because of all these things, then we're going to be accepted.

So we're saying to them, the point of all this is that we're coming empty handed. And God wants us to recognize and to accept and to own the emptiness and to say, "If anything is going to be good, if anything's valuable, if I'm going to be saved in any way, it's coming from what You've done, not from what I'm bringing into the equation." So we're trying to constantly have the sense where we're communicating the complete and total and utter sufficiency for Christ for everything. From salvation to life, to being the Source of everything it is that you do.

This again comes back in Ephesians and in Romans and all these sorts of things where you see Scripture saying, "Okay, in light of all of this, now, therefore..." And then there's some appeal to action. But that appeal to action is always coming after a grounding in a relationship and an understanding of the wholeness and completeness and the sufficiency of this relationship. And it's the outflow of that relationship that now says, "Now, therefore..." And you get into practical matters of, "Don't do this, or this, or the other thing." But it's always that sense of tying it back to who God is first rather than starting from the idea of, "Let's make these following adjustments."

John gives an example of a woman who evaluates her actions according to the Spirit's guidance rather than by cultural norms:

I remember once, we had the field chairman come in, and I was telling him about all these amazing changes that we're seeing in the lives of these people. And we hadn't even got into the New Testament. And we walked down to what we call their teaching house, which was just a big roof but could accommodate about 250 people actually and get them in out of the sun or out of the rain.

As we came off the road or off the track and into the teaching house, there I see this woman bashing the daylights out of this young girl. And I've just been raving on about how wonderful these people are and we're confronted with this sight. Anyway, we come over and we're able to see that thing stopped. There just seemed to be dramas all the time in there, but those things were changing and I thought, "What a shame we saw this after I've told him all that other stuff. It's unfortunate that he's not probably going to get a very good picture of what is actually happening here."

The woman that was beating that young girl, she was the daughter of the patriarch actually for that area. She could be a very mean woman. She'd gone through two or three husbands and I'd heard stories that she'd beaten her husband and all sorts of things. She could be a very mean woman. That afternoon, that woman came up to my house and said to me, "Sita Larry," (that's what they called me which was the way they pronounced "Australia" initially). She says, "Sita Larry, I was right to punish her because she stole from my garden." Basically what I said to her was, "If that's the way you guys deal with theft and that's your system of social control and you know for sure that she did you wrong, then yes, okay fair enough."

She said, "That's right." She went away. She came back the next day and she said, "Sita Larry, I did do right, did I? I did do right to beat that girl." I said,

"That's the way you guys deal with theft, yes. You probably did." Off she went again.

The next morning, that young girl and her husband came to our house and they said, "Do you know what happened? That woman came to me and she apologized. She told me how sorry she was for beating me. And she said she has never apologized, she has never admitted ever doing anything wrong ever in her entire life. And yet she came and she apologized." These were the sorts of things that we were seeing happening. People were changing before our very eyes.

Kaikou says that before they were born again, death was a terrible thing to them, but now when believers pass away it is a totally different thing:

> I want to talk about the life of the church. It is like before we heard God's Word we were alive but in a way we were dead. That goes right back to our ancestors and came right through to our generation before we believed. We understand now that we, like all humans, were dead because we were separated from God's life.
>
> And so it dates back to the beginning when people began to live on the earth. They were physically alive but spiritually dead. In the past, when death came into our communities, our mourning was extreme. We didn't understand death at all. And at times like that, we would be terrified because we would think, "When you die, what happens?" Fear really gripped us often when we thought about the issue of death and where we would go when we died.
>
> But once we heard about Christ, and we put our faith in Him, we knew that we were restored to the source of life Himself. And now it brings us incredible joy to know that we are connected directly to Christ as individuals and also as a group. Even at times of sickness now, instead of being terrified we are joyful because we remember our lives are joined to Christ life. If death happens, we cry but we don't mourn like we used to. Now, we know that our bodies go into the earth but our spirits will live on and so we have a sense of joy along with the sorrow.

From the last case study we saw that death is such a terrible thing for those who don't know the Lord. The unsaved are full of hopelessness because they'll never again see the person who died. But when they come to Christ, as Kaikou described in the last example, the change is vividly apparent because they know Him and now when they face things as terrible as death, it's actually something that can be mixed with joy. They're not going to see that person again on this earth, but they will see them in heaven and they have that hope which makes all the difference.

God wants us to see our new lives in Christ become a reality. The Spirit of Christ in us. Think of that in contrast to the Pharisees. Jesus was speaking about the Pharisees and condemning them because they got it backwards. They actually tried to produce the life from the outside and get their conduct on the facades perfected. But Jesus is saying that even though you might look nice on the outside, like really whitewashed, but on the inside you might actually be full of dead men's bones. This was quite disgusting. Dead men's bones defiled things in the Old Testament. Jesus is wanting the Pharisees to have the life that stems from within and then that in turn changes the outward parts.

? DISCUSSION POINTS

1. As you listen to the church planters in this tutorial, make note of anything they mention that were key indicators of the believers' deepening relationship with the Lord Jesus.

2. Imagine you have had opportunity to share God's Word in a minority group, where music is only used in traditional rituals. The new believers begin to write songs of worship and they ask you if it is OK to accompany these songs using their traditional instruments and music style. How would you respond?

9.14 The purpose for which we exist

> **OBJECTIVES OF THIS TUTORIAL**
>
> This tutorial looks at the second question under the area of Life: 'Are they gaining clarity about the true purpose for which they exist, and are they increasingly able to identify those things that hinder their life in Christ?'

Philippians 3:10: I want to know Christ and experience the mighty power that raised him from the dead. I want to suffer with him, sharing in his death.

In this passage you can see Paul's heart in that he realises death is necessary and that he needs to be associated with Christ in His death in order for life to come forth. There's actually an outworking that God wants to happen from that life, that we move towards something; there's actually a direction in which He wants us to head, and it's not just to maintain the status quo.

Even in the realm of a church, a group of God's people who somehow have that as their heartbeat, it's not just about maintaining or building up the church. It exists for a purpose and that involves death. It's kind of ironic or a paradox that when we talk about life and the plan of redemption, we also talk about death in the same breath. There's no other way to have that life apart from that, as Christ demonstrated for us so clearly.

Last time

We looked at the first question from the WILD outline in the area of Life. We talked about people having a deepening relationship with Jesus and how that results in changes in their values and behavior. In this tutorial we will discuss the second question in the WILD outline in the area of Life.

Are they gaining clarity about the true purpose for which they exist, and are they increasingly able to identify those things that hinder their life in Christ?

THE PURPOSE FOR WHICH WE EXIST

We asked Philip and Kaikou what they see as being their purpose here on earth, as a church in that community:

> The source of this new life that we received came through faith in what Christ has done for us. When we were saved God didn't take us out of the earth. He left us here to demonstrate this new life to others, to those who are still in their old life and do not know Him. He has given His work to the church: to take His truth out to those who are still in darkness, and for us to teach God's Word to them so that they can know Him and enjoy new life as well. He wants us to live so that we can encourage one another as believers. Jesus was our example of Someone who revealed God to others and gave His life for the church.
>
> The reason we are here is to represent Christ and that is something that we are thrilled about. We know that the new life that we have isn't going to finish because that comes from the Lord Himself. In our past lives we tried to do things but they really came to nothing. All the religious activity we did, we complained about and we wearied of it, but not now. Whatever work we do to strengthen the body or to extend His church, we are really enjoying it. We are happy to do it because He has given us this new life. Now God has given us the strength and ability to do His work and that is wonderful.

Do they have a growing desire to understand why God has placed them in their particular place and time?

Phil describes a growing understanding among the new believers of themselves within God's larger plan:

> As we talk about that we say, "This is what God's saving you towards, being useful, and this is what He's demonstrating of Himself—drawing people to Himself." Part of His drawing people to Himself is to show what He's accomplished through what He's done. All that is part of this thing that He's drawing us into and wants us to understand and be a part of. The believers, as they get into this, are recognising, "You know what? It's not only my job to go through the day and just survive...the Lord has me here for a purpose. He wants what I'm doing. He wants to use me for whatever He's weaving together there, and one of the primary aspects of that is my own conformity to Him and the conformity of us as a group of believers to Him."
>
> In Ephesians there's this imagery of the bride and the husband on their wedding day. The bride has put in quite a big investment of her own, you know, how she dresses and how this thing happens because she wants to look

her best. We're trying to take that and use the imagery that is there and say, "This is what God's trying to do ... He's working, in the sense of conforming us, towards this ideal that He has. He's moving our collective and individual growth towards Him. It's resulting in this thing that closer resembles who He is. So His purity and all of these things—His righteousness, His perfection—that's what He's moving us towards individually and collectively."

As they are beginning to see, "Oh this is why God saved me. He's saving me because He's in this process of conforming me and us into something, and not just us, but also the believers that are in this village, all of us that are believers here and all of us that are believers anywhere in the world at this given time, and also any believers over the course of time and into the future."
For them to be sensing that as they go through Scripture, it's almost like the Lord keeps stretching how far they're seeing and how far they're recognising the implications of this. It's been cool to see them start to recognise, "We're brothers with these guys. We're brothers with guys in any other place. God's working and He's doing all this for this corporate sense and He's moving us towards Him and transforming us into His image, and that's important to Him."

Is their perspective of why they exist being shaped by God's Word, His view of their Identity, and by the Discipleship relationship they have with Jesus Christ?

Phil describes the process of cultural change taking place in the community:

In terms of seeing them look at cultural practices and then go, "Wait a second here, if this is true, this over here can't be true." With these clan leaders, who are really the core of the religious system, there's a veneer of Islam, but it's really these clan leaders and their relationship to the ancestors that is the core of the culture. These clan leaders, like I said before, we have quite a few of them attending the teaching and there's an abnormally high number of these guys relative to the population who are believers and growing in that. They've seen different things that stand out to them that say, "You know what, you can't keep doing this."

One of the situations that particularly stands out to me is these guys doing flour ceremonies. It's grain that they'll take to a tree and they'll sprinkle it on the ground. They'll take two handfuls of it and they'll drop it onto this little pile and they'll invoke the spirits. This is what they always used to do. When Islam came there was pressure from Islam to put God high, so they changed their ceremonies to start off with, "In the name of God who's most magnificent and kind," a typical Arabic reading, and then they would go into, "And now ancestors so and so, and ancestors so and so." It was simply a quick little cover for making these guys happy, to start off by asking Allah for this, "And now we're going get into the real ancestors."

One of the guys, he's from the most important clan, from the first clan to arrive here so he's dominant. Even if you're not from his clan you have to invoke the name of his clan's ancestors in any of your prayers. He's this dominant figure in the community and he started coming to the teaching and he started listening. Pretty early on, even before he was a believer, he was starting to recognize, "Hmm, the things that I'm saying are not true. I'm invoking spirits for help that can't help me and they aren't the most powerful spirits out there."

As time went on he became a believer. He's in charge of these flour ceremonies, he starts them and he ends them. He's the most important figure in the whole ceremony. He starts doing these ceremonies and he won't name an ancestor, he only prays to God. Then the next guy comes, the next more important person and it just goes down by level of importance until you get regular guys who want to do, they do it, and then that guy who started it comes back and wraps it up again. They were at the ceremony, and I was there listening to it. I've got it recorded. He's going through this whole thing where he's talking to God. The next guy happened to be a believer as well and they talked to God. Then a lot of the other guys that came, there was this mixture, probably a third of them were believers who wouldn't name an ancestor, and the other guys were naming ancestors. Then he comes back again, finishes it up and doesn't name an ancestor.

Somebody yelled from the back of the crowd as he finished up, they're like, "Aren't you going to name an ancestor, at least one?" He yells back—I don't know whether he knew who it was that said it or not—he said, "If I thought they could do something I'd pray to them, but I don't think they can do anything so I won't. I'm only going to pray to the One that actually can do something." That was his public response. There were all sorts of murmurings and carrying on as everybody dispersed at the end of that ceremony because of what he said. That's his job. He exists to be the link between the living members of this clan and the dead members of this clan. He's been given this responsibility... he wears a special hat, he gets special greetings, he has special taboos. It's kind of like the pope not doing mass. You're the most important guy who deals with the most important ancestors in this whole community, how is it that you're not appealing to them and not only not appealing, but in a public way saying, "I'm not going to do that"?

In my mind that's the sort of stuff that's sending the shock waves. We spend quite a bit of time on the identity side talking about Islam because that's what sticks out to us, that's what we see as what's most important. But if you're actually looking at what holds this culture together, it's the ancestor side that's much more pivotal to the whole thing. We're coming to guys and we're saying, "What about life?", in the sense of when you die, what's going to happen, all this sort of stuff. If it's talking about going to Heaven or not going to Heaven, those are moot points, like who cares? Those aren't big deals. What's going to happen down in the future is, "I'm worried about right now, shortly after death, what's going to happen with all the ancestors and my spirit? That's the thing I'm worried about. I'm not really worried about day of judgement and whether there's eternal fire or not. I hear that from these religions, but that's not what worries me. That's not what keeps me up at night. What keeps me up at night is all these powers and whether my life force is being sucked away or not." They're the issues that are there. The spirit realm and the ancestor realm are the primary movers and shakers in that department.

This guy and a whole bunch of others perform rain ceremonies. It wasn't raining a few months ago and the amount of pressure that's on these guys to do these rain ceremonies is huge and a bunch of them, because they're believers, are resisting the rain ceremony or trying to modify the rain ceremony in some way to keep it from violating their consciousness. It was pretty cool to watch them go through that process.

Are they learning to evaluate, with God's help, how well they are fitting into the purposes God has for them, the immediate challenges they face, and the areas that need to be adjusted to fulfill those purposes?

Kaikou talks about the fact that, in this present life, sin is a constant reality that has to be dealt with appropriately in the church:

> I wanted to add to what I was saying about our life in Christ. Like I said before, we are here on this earth and that's the way it is because God wants us here, but along with that is the presence of sin that we can't escape from now. Sometimes we are not strong enough to resist sin and we do things that we know are wrong, and we are surprised at ourselves that it still happens. In the past we didn't recognize sin for what it is, but in our new lives it has become really important to us to not get involved in things that we know to be wrong. The reason is that we see those things are obstacles to our growth,

our lives, and our relationship with Jesus. We regularly talk about that with Him because we know that those things are not what He wants for us. We try to be open about those things with Him and apologize because we know that they really don't help our life and walk with Him.

Now Kaikou talks about a situation that he and the other elders dealt with and the steps that they took:

> Another thing that relates to the life of church is when someone has been involved in something wrong for some time. I am talking about something that the individual refuses to recognize and that is affecting the entire body in that place. We are reminded in those cases of the situation in the Corinth where there was a very serious moral issue going on within the church. The Apostle Paul instructed them to deal with that issue and we take that very seriously in the life of the church here because we are conscious that sin like that can become a real obstacle to the life of the church. In cases like that, we follow a process to deal with the situation because not dealing with someone carefully like that is not showing love to that brother who has been involved in sin.

> I am reminded of a real-life example that involved a young man. He got involved in something very wrong on one occasion and we worked with him to see it rectified. But he showed a lack of awe for God and he went back and did the same thing again. We went to him and tried to help him recognize it for what it was, but he refused. Then we went about dealing with the situation like this, one thing was that he was a worker in the church. He was a literacy teacher. We had sent him as part of our new outreach team. We began to follow the process the Bible lays out because we value our new life so much.

> We went ahead and brought him back to his original sending church community. We spoke clearly to him and the matter was also made clear to all our ten community churches. We said that the church had put him outside its fellowship. Of course that had a profound effect on the young man, but also on all the churches. He was put out like that and it was difficult, but he gained a great deal in his life through that process. It helped us to gain insights from God's Word and we saw an even deeper respect for God's authority through that situation. The young man was eventually able to return under the protection of the fellowship and the nourishment of God's Word.

In the case study above, Kaikou eluded to a situation where a young man was taken back to his sending church. But he wasn't taken in chains. There was no one forcing him; he submitted to the authority of the leaders. This was the first time anything like this occurred in the church there. It was a significant thing at the time and also in the history of the church because of the way it was dealt with. It really served as an example of dealing with things that hinder the life of the church.

The young man went back to his home village which was high up on a mountain ridge. He walked into the village under these circumstances of church discipline. He walked up the middle of the village and people were crying and weeping. No one came out as they normally would when someone comes home to their village, they just stood there and watched him walk up to his father's house. It was a real sense of devastation, that someone they'd sent out for the work of the church was now coming back under these circumstances. It had a huge impact in that village and the other village churches.

To cut a long story short, a couple of months later, Kaikou, who has a real discipleship heart, came and got the young man and took him to the village where he lived. There was a small hut next to his house. The young man lived in that house for a number of months and Kaikou went through God's Word with him, helping him to understand how to deal with his sin. They started in Romans. A year later, he was restored and had a part again in the outreach and today is married and is a significant part of the church. It is a beautiful story of actually loving a brother who has fallen into sin.

In each of the case studies in this tutorial, we saw that God's intent for the church is to exist with purpose. It's not just to exist. We need to look at things that might hinder us and not just gloss them over. Instead of saying, "Those are his problems, not my problems," we can start recognizing, "We're together, a body, and God wants our body to be used for His glory to actually reach out to others." We need to see anything that might hinder that as something we should deal with, and we should deal with it in a loving way so that the person can be healed and we can function and exist and do the things that God is wanting for us.

ACTIVITIES

1. In a few paragraphs identify some of the key elements and events that shaped a growing understanding of God's specific purposes for the early church in Acts. Comment on how that account might relate to a new church in a minority group today.

9.15 Understanding God's purposes

 OBJECTIVES OF THIS TUTORIAL

This tutorial looks at the third question under the area of Life: 'Are they increasingly able to make good decisions based on their understanding of God's local and global purposes, and to use their time, money and other resources accordingly?'

2 Corinthians 4:7: We now have this light shining in our hearts, but we ourselves are like fragile clay jars containing this great treasure. This makes it clear that our great power is from God, not from ourselves.

Another way Paul describes that treasure is actually like gold glimmering or something shining out from our hearts. And that's why we're talking about life here shining out. It doesn't stay within. But what is that supposed to look like? What is God's intent for us individually and as a body of believers? And how can that be replicated in other locations where that as yet does not exist?

When we see God's Word going out in a fellowship, it's a sign of health and a sign that people are truly understanding why they exist, why they're being given this life. They are to enjoy it and see the body built up for sure, but then they're to see it go out and be made available to others.

Last time

We looked at the second question from the WILD outline in the area of Life. It talked about people gaining clarity about the true purpose for which they exist and if they are able to identify hindrances to their life in Christ. In this tutorial we will discuss the third question in the WILD outline in the area of Life.

Are they increasingly able to make good decisions based on their understanding of God's local and global purposes, and to use their time, money and other resources accordingly?

Are they learning to recognize how personal and cultural preferences can exert a subtle but powerful influence on the directions their choices take them?

Palava shares her thoughts about moving house regularly as a part of her ministry with her husband:

> When we heard the truth, I was just still a baby in the faith, but then another village came and asked us to come and teach them God's Word. Kaikou, my husband, came to ask me about it. It was very difficult for me, my garden was there, my house, our relatives. But he said, "We are going to pull down our house and move to a new village." So I went and read in God's Word where our Lord says, "Go our into the world and take My Word and teach it to people." So I said to myself, "Yes, that true."
>
> God's Word is more important than my village or my garden or any other thing. So I put aside my own desires about life in my village and stepped out on the path to that new village who had called us to teach them. Then we began our new life there. I had to put aside all the things I wanted to hold on to from my old life. Because I knew God was leading us and holding is in His hand. So we moved and lived in that village and did God's work there and I saw that we were in God's hand. He looked after us, He guided us, He helped us in the work, He helped us in our lives—He did everything.
>
> So I lift up the name of our Creator, because after we left our home, I changed the way I thought about what life was all about. He helped me to see what the truly important things are. I want to use my life for His work.

Does their decision-making process involve them regularly asking God how He wants to involve them in the things He's doing in their immediate vicinity and beyond?

Phil talks about how access to God's narrative is providing an increasing clarity about purpose for the body of believers:

> There's been a growing understanding of purpose. I would say first of all, by listening to God's Word, there has been the introduction of a purpose. I think a lot of the turmoil in the culture was the lack of purpose, or the lack of a clear purpose. The way cultures are shifting, and there's so many different voices speaking into cultures these days, that functionally for a lot of people there is no cohesion in any of the stuff that they believe. They've got such a mixture of different religions and different traditional stuff. Even the pressure from a communist school system saying there is no God. And so

they've got this kind of mix of stories, so many different stories, they pick a thing or two from each different story or whatever seems most convenient at the time. They don't have a cohesive sense of, "This is why we're here, this is what's happening, this is why things are the way they are and this is where it's going." So the teaching of Scripture has been providing for them this sense of this meta-narrative. It's providing for them, I think for the first time, a cohesive sense of what happened, why did it get started in the first place, why are things the way they are now and where all this is going.

So as you see them placing themselves and seeing themselves in the storyline it's providing for them a greater and greater sense of purpose that God put us here to show people what it's like to demonstrate who He is and He actually wants to work that through us. They can say, "I'm here to show people what God is like." We spent quite a bit of time on being made in God's image and what that means. It's not talking about a physical body, it's talking about His characteristics. And now as we're moving forward we're starting to tie that in. We haven't come to Galatians with the fruit of the Spirit, like we haven't got there in terms of teaching that verse yet or translating that verse yet. But when we get there they're going to immediately recognize it because that's been the theme of what we've been doing all along; that God who is these things, when that God controls us, when that God sends us to do His bidding and to be His hands and His feet, those are characteristics that belong to Him. The peace and the love and the long-suffering and all these things are what He wants us to demonstrate to other people.

Palava explains how the women in the church saw a need for regular times of prayer and fellowship:

> We recognize that as women there is a real need to get together and encourage one another in our faith. And so we regularly get together to share areas of need in our lives and to pray for one another and to ask for God's help with our children and families. We also tried to organize to help in practical ways in the community. For example if the old people's house needs fixing or if they are short of firewood we discuss about how we can meet those needs that we see and we organize ourselves to meet those needs. And that has been good fruit for me. It has been a source of real joy to the women to serve in this way together.

UNDERSTANDING GOD'S PURPOSES

Ela talks about how the women in the churches saw a need to provide food for large groups of visitors, and they organized themselves to meet it:

> The thing we women are involved in the most in God's work in the church in terms of the body of Christ is in supporting God's work. We women help in various ways, providing food and other practical aspects of helping with large events. We are conscious of God's grace in our lives so our response is to support His work. We understand that this is one of our roles in God's work. When there are large Bible teacher's meetings, we all help according to our abilities. We all share what food we have and we are grateful that God gives us the skills and abilities to be able to serve like that. We ask God to help us know how to run these big events and to do the work really well. We women are delighted that God has shown us how to do things properly and we get a lot of joy from it. We see spiritual fruit among us women and it also comes out as practical help for the church.

Palava adds to what Ela said about the women's ministry by describing where they find their motivation:

> It really goes back to the things the apostles were talking about in the past and how they organized themselves to give practical help to the church. They define specific roles for those who would do that. So we took that example and we looked at the abilities God has given to us women and we concluded that God had indeed given us skills and abilities to use. We're grateful to the Lord to work together like that because we never experienced this kind of cooperation and unity in our lives before.

Is their relationship with Jesus and growing familiarity with His perspectives having an observable impact on major life-changing decisions as well as every day priorities and choices?

Gebi talks about how the believers are much more aware of prioritizing the things of God and trusting him with their work, finances and everyday lives:

> The reason God wants us to live on earth is to demonstrate Christ's life to others. In the past we did what we felt like doing. That is what everyone was occupied with and what they were consumed with. There was no real purpose for doing anything we did. Now we see believers building things that are about the work of church. Before if we earnt some money we would just use it to please ourselves. But now, having understood God's grace, we also understand the reason God wants us to live out our lives on the earth: to reveal His life and to participate in His work. One way that we do contribute to God's

work is to use the money that comes into our hands for His purposes. We all join together in giving as a group.

We began this tutorial with the question, "Are they increasingly able to make good decisions based on their understanding of God's local and global purposes and to use their time, money and resources accordingly?" And Gebi described how they used to use their money on themselves. And now they're actually 180 degrees the opposite of that. And why is that? It's because Christ is in them. And we saw the way Jesus thought as He lived on this earth, the way He spoke and what He prioritized. John 15:4 says, "Abide in me and I in you as a branch cannot bear fruit by itself unless it abides in a vine. Neither can you unless you abide in me." And so we see the source of life and the importance of that connection to that vine. When we're connected, then fruit can come from that and people can be impacted and lives change, like we saw in the case studies above.

 DISCUSSION POINTS

1. In the tutorial video one of the ladies talked about her willingness to be uprooted and to move home regularly for the sake of God's work. What are your thoughts on living that kind of lifestyle, and of the possibility of living in a different country?

1. Specifically with church planting in view, share your thoughts on the following areas:

a) Appropriate roles for women in the church and in its outreach.

b) Raising outside finances to help the church in disadvantaged areas of the world.

9.16 Form, function, fulfilment

✓ OBJECTIVES OF THIS TUTORIAL

This tutorial looks at the fourth question under the area of Life: 'Are they learning to shape the form of what they do to serve whatever function they are convinced will lead to the fulfilment of God's objectives?

> 1 Corinthians 12:6: God works in different ways, but it is the same God who does the work in all of us.

Last time

We looked at the third question from the WILD outline in the area of Life. We focused on how people use their resources based on their understanding of God's purposes, both locally and globally. In this tutorial we will discuss the fourth question in the WILD outline in the area of Life.

We'll look at the areas of form and function, with the ultimate goal of fulfilling or seeing what God does and being part of that. Form needs to serve function, but so often it gets reversed, doesn't it? It happens especially in religion and in a lot of the ministry contexts we see. But we know in the New Testament that He doesn't legislate much form really. We know that the believers met regularly, but a lot of forms and details about the Lord's Supper, or baptism, aren't legislated.

The verse above is freeing. When we go into different ministry contexts and cultures, we don't need to bring some particular form and awkwardly try to fit it into their context. We actually have all kinds of freedom because God works in different ways.

That's quite a contrast to what religion often brings, as many have forms of Christianity, but without life. They may be doing the forms of meeting together on Sundays, and having baptisms and communion, and all the things on the outside maybe look okay. To an untrained eye it would look authentic. But it doesn't mean there's life. And it's not God's intent to just follow these forms, but instead, the forms need to be coming out of life, meeting a real function, and when the function exists then the forms will then serve that. The real life of the church is generated by Christ Himself. The truth teaches and the Spirit guides us as to how we are to develop those forms in each setting.

Are they learning to shape the form of what they do to serve whatever function they are convinced will lead to the fulfillment of God's objectives?

Are they seeing that God is not interested in empty, static, religious tradition but in something living, authentic and richly diverse?

Phil describes how the church planting team was careful to address in their teaching, the difference between real life and religious tradition:

> Tracing through history, the Lord has always had true believers. That's been important for us to communicate, partly because in terms of identity we're trying to stay separate from some of the denominational churches that are around here, and we're trying to say actually, "We want you to recognize that the Lord has always had His true believers, and there's always been groups that have often lost the core essence."
>
> So when we're talking about the church, we don't use those terms. We don't say, "the church", we say, "the body of believers". They all associate the church with, say, the Catholic Church. So we're trying to keep some distance between this word that they're familiar with called "church" and what we're talking about. So we're trying to highlight that all through history, the Lord has had His people that believe the truth, that follow Him, that trust Him, but around that has grown up all of this religion.
>
> And so what we're trying to say is that even though these guys say and do all these things that we're going to read about in Scripture, oftentimes it's simply a shell. It's a veneer, but they've lost the inner meaning of the thing. So they're going to bring up, let's say baptism, and they're going to say that baptism is what brings you salvation. It's the process that you go through for salvation. And we're saying that baptism's actually a sign of something that goes down in your heart. It's an outward sign. Because people can't see your heart, the Lord is giving you an opportunity to publicly say to people, "This is where my heart's gone. This is what it believes, and I'm doing this act as a public testimony to what you guys can't see in my heart."
>
> And so we're saying, "You're going to see, now, all of these different groups taking elements of the truth, doing all sorts of right stuff, but it's not actually connected to the heart of the issue that God has in mind. And so we want

you to know that we're constantly bringing you back to the fact that this is the true thing as revealed in His Word. This is the heart of the matter, and even though you're going to see all this stuff, what you're looking to connect with is not with this group or that group or the other group. You're looking to connect with those people that understand and accept this core part of truth, and the Lord has always had those people throughout the whole of history. And even in these other groups in different places, you're going to find people that believe and hold to these things because they've heard from God's Word the truth. And so we're wanting you to build relationships with those guys, wherever you find them, and recognize that the Lord has always been at work and always has them. Now you guys are a part of that."

Phil talks about how the believers need to focus on God and his purposes as they develop forms:

They're asking us constantly, "Tell us what the book says. Pull out the Book. And what does it say about Scripture?" And it blows their mind that you can't have a chapter and verse that says, "When the person dies, then say this, wash them in this way, face them this direction, do this," all the stuff that they're used to doing. It blows their mind that there's nothing in Scripture that explains in detail how a believer's supposed to be baptized, and we keep coming back to this idea that it's because God's not interested in giving us all of these details of what to do, as if He's going to give us a new religion. He's wanting us to understand the heart of the thing, the function so to speak, and not get caught up in the form of the thing.

And so, in that sense, the struggle is constantly trying to bring them back to the sense of connection to who He is, and the sense of life, and the sense of His complete sufficiency and not in focusing on things that we do. Focusing on things that we do, but not because that earns us anything, but because that's what God saved us for: to be able to use us for His purposes. So He wants to use us for His purposes.

Bill and Kelley describe how the New Testament model was foundational as the church planting team and the believers saw forms for teaching, prayer and community meetings develop:

I think as we were right there at the start of the brand-new church and thinking through how we were going to set things up, we were committed of course to making sure that this model would follow a New Testament model rather than putting our own cultural thoughts and ideas into how this would look.

One of the things we realized early on though is that to give them nothing is to give them a form. And what ends up happening is (and it happened to us) that everybody tends to sit around like in a church service if you don't give it any form. Everybody tends to sit around and stare at each other. Just like you do with your kids, it's important to look at them in a young state, and then as they start growing, be sure that you're evaluating what you're doing and giving more freedom as they grow.

So early on, we didn't try to give them any strict model to follow. We did give them a lot of freedom in how they were going to do the teaching, how they were going to sing, how they were going to pray in the services, how they were going to interact with each other as a community, even the number of times per week that they were going to get together and meet together. We didn't prescribe that, but we helped them work through that, and put some ideas down for them to help them walk through that.

Then as the church grew, one of the things that we did was try to help them evaluate. And in the culture that we work in, evaluating is a big no-no. You just let things go. But they actually learned to love it, in the sense of being able to stop as teachers and as believers and think through what they've done. Okay, how can we do this better? Not that we will become a stronger, better church on the outside, but that we would glorify the Lord in what we were doing.

And that really began to be the drumbeat, it was like, "Okay, we're here to glorify the Lord in everything we're doing. How does that look then in the teaching?" The teaching was longer, and I remember one of the elders was sitting there with a watch one time, and evaluating one of the guys that was teaching, and he was writing times down on the lesson paper that we had. And then afterwards all the teachers always get together and go through the evaluation period of the service that we just had. And he was just talking about how people in the congregation were falling asleep and he was already at the 45-minute mark. And just again, this was not to be ugly, or to put him down, but to just help him be a teacher that could be a good shepherd to these people that were trying to hear and understand the Word of God.

And we saw that on a number of different occasions. I remember too, some of the songs that they were singing. As we started singing them, we realized, and some of the teachers realized that some of the songs weren't glorifying to the Lord but they tended to be more praising man and what he had done.

And so they took those out of the church and wouldn't let those be sung in the church.

So again, you're helping them with form a little bit, so that they can get started, but then the further they go along, making sure that you're standing further back from that and letting things happen according to what fits their culture. But then, of course through that, remember that you need to make sure that glorifying the Lord is the goal, not to try and make this church service run smooth, or anything like that.

It has to be connected with that. They have to see the reason for wanting to evaluate is that the message is heard more clearly, that people understand and then it actually works through that function out into the fulfilment of everyday life where they're actually practicing that. And they can't practice that if they're falling asleep because the guy is going so long. So, we realized that it takes a little form. Our God is the God of order. He's not a God of chaos, so there has to be some kind of order and form that they can follow. But it doesn't have to be our form. It can be something that is indigenous to them, that they're comfortable with.

So what they've practically fallen into now, how that has evolved and what they do is, they have a general greeting time. They have a short prayer, and then they do some singing. They usually sing for maybe 20 minutes or so. And then they have a time of prayer. So they usually take prayer requests from the congregation, and then whoever has had that prayer request will also pray for it. So they'll take five or six prayer requests and then they'll start their time of prayer.

And actually something that they added in was a journal. So someone is marked, one of the deacons is marked every week, and he writes down these prayer requests. Because they felt like the Lord was answering prayer requests, and they were forgetting what had happened, or just not acknowledging or giving thanks for that. So somebody writes down the prayer requests, they pray for those, and then they just have a time of thanksgiving. And actually this is my favorite time of the whole church service, because it's just so good to see what's in their hearts, what's happened that week, and what the Lord has been showing them.

And it will be things from providing food, or a mishap maybe that turned out okay, or someone being healed from malaria or whatever. But then also to the spiritual things, where they're saying, "I'm so thankful that we are one in Christ, and that our friends over there now have heard the Gospel that we're all one family." It goes on maybe for 20 minutes as well. And then they move into the actual teaching time. After the teaching time then they close in prayer, and then they have questions if there's questions.

Bill and Kelley discuss the process of the development for forms for Communion and the church meetings:

> Another example is Communion. When that came up they wanted to know about it. We don't tell them, "You need to be baptized. You need to have Communion. Do these things." As you're teaching through Acts, they just come up and they say, "Well, should we still be doing that today?" And we're like, "Yeah, we should." So you move onto that next thing.
>
> And with Communion, they asked, "How often do we do it?" And so we were able just to lay out, "Well some people say this often, once a month. Some people say every week. Some people say once a quarter. I'm sure some people do it once a year. It's just that it doesn't tell us exactly what it is." And so they met together and decided they were going to do it once a month, and that was their decision how they were going to do that. Their reasoning was because it takes a lot of work to get the bread and the coconut, and they didn't want to give the women a big hard job of doing that every week. So that's why they decided to do it once a month.
>
> Yeah, and so they also do it with coconut water so it looks very different. But I love it. I love Communion at our place, because it's not chaos, but it's very much interactive. And so people are getting their glasses, and everybody brings their own little cup, and some of them just have lids, and some of them are sharing cups, and the elders are like, "Does everybody have some?" Or the deacons, "Everybody have some?" And then it settles back down and then they pray, and then another round of it.

Are they learning to see threads in God's Narrative and to draw current applications of how He leads His people to develop forms for their function that are appropriate to the time and place?

Greg explains how the form of group meetings developed and was shaped by the believers and the culture and context there:

> In Siberia, because of the conditions and the life that you live in, you don't meet outside, you don't meet in places that are social gatherings. You meet in houses. And it's one of the most common things to meet in apartments or in houses and that's where you gather together.

> So the group began first off just in homes, where people would just gather together in homes, fellowshipping together. Church began in the homes. And as the churches began to grow, as the groups began to develop more and more connection with one another, we had five or six or seven different groups that were existing in people's homes, and they wanted to get to know each other. They wanted to get to know who they were as a body of believers. They wanted to get to understand who each other was.
>
> And so we talked about a broader meeting space, a place where we could gather together, where we could actually function together and actually experience life with each other. And so the believers found a facility that we could meet in, where we gathered together and it was during the week. It was an evening during the week where we gathered together, we broke bread, we prayed together, and we had teachings going on. And the format or the style of the church was developed by the believers in the way that they felt was most comfortable to them, which identified with them. Dancing was a very big part of what they were going to do, and so they actually did their worship dances that they would do, and that was important to them to have that a part of it. It was important for them to have prayer. They felt that that was a significant part of it.
>
> We took a lot of it, as we studied through the book of Acts and how the church existed, and as they began to see the characteristics of the church body. Meeting together, breaking bread together, praying together and teaching the Word together is what they wanted to do as a body. And they've continued that to this day.

Philip talks about how the worship, teaching and meeting forms have developed as they came to understand more of God's Word and how God's Word has the primary place at meetings:

> Once we had a relationship with Christ, we began to meet together as groups of His children. We didn't just automatically adopt the religious forms that we had seen elsewhere, whether that be the way that we met together or sing or pray. We looked to God's Word to guide us. It's not just a role of a few leaders to run everything, for example. Others have responsibility for music, and other areas, or with prayer. It is not just the elders who do that in the church gatherings, because the body is made up of many different parts. That is reflected in the way the meetings are run.
>
> So when we pray, or sing, then lots of different people contribute, because God has given those responsibilities to the whole body, not just a few. The

gathering is an extension of what the Spirit is doing in the lives of His people all the time. So the prayers of the believers, or the songs that are sung, reflect the true life of the church, and the teaching of God's Word of course is a big part of it. But the most important thing is being conscious that the gathering should be about Christ Himself and His grace. And because He is holy, then we should really take seriously this time of coming together as His body, and we shouldn't do things in a chaotic way, or bring things that are not profitable. We need to do things that remind people of the relationship that they actually have with God, and we have to avoid bringing into the church things from the wider culture, that are not pleasing to God.

Are they open to the Spirit's guidance and input from others as they regularly evaluate and adjust their activities to serve the church and facilitate its witness?

Dave tells of how the believers changed in their approach to music:

> Traditionally, when the people sang, they would play their drums and they would sing traditional songs. When they came to know the Lord they carried some of those over, and created many, many Christian songs, even with their traditional drums. But they knew that there were certain drumbeats that they would not use for a Christian song. There's no way that we would have been able to make that assessment. To us, we might be able to distinguish that this is one drumbeat, this is another one, but we would have no idea which ones would be ones that should not be used, that would not be appropriate, for use with Christian songs.
>
> They clearly knew that. They got together, they discussed it, they decided upon which drumbeats. And in fact it was quite easy for them to come to consensus on it. They seemed to all know that these particular drumbeats needed to be left behind, needed to be forgotten as a former part of their culture, and these others were acceptable and appropriate for Christian songs.

Dave describes how existing cultural forms of meeting became times of fellowship:

> Also with these cultural celebrations that they used to have, which really were designed to raise the status of the leader men, the village elders, they found other reasons to get together. They would come together, sometimes maybe at Easter time, or at other times that weren't even for a particular holiday. And they would have food and times of fellowship, times of teaching together with people from other villages, and as I said, sometimes people even from other language groups would come. There was a felt need for them to have people from various villages get together.

And that's not a bad thing in and of itself. And it was very encouraging to see them still coming together as villages, but now these village celebrations are centered on lifting up God's name rather than lifting up the name of one of the village leaders.

Bill describes the church planter's dilemma in guiding the believers as they develop forms:

> I think in the church service specifically, it does depend on the group that you have. If you have a larger group, you have to introduce form a lot sooner, because it's just going to be chaotic if you don't. But as a good church planter, you just need to be wise as to when to start backing off and letting them pour into that, rather than you giving them ideas. It's just a matter of learning to adjust with them, always evaluating yourself, just like we always ask them to evaluate themselves.

In this tutorial we started with the question, "Are they learning to shape the form of what they do to serve whatever function they are convinced will lead to the fulfilment of God's objectives?" The form must be based on the function, and the function in turn must be based on fulfilling what God wants. People so often want to prioritize the form and make it the most important thing, and it's often associated with salvation itself. But these forms actually come after salvation, and they are supposed to help believers fulfill what God has for them.

As we look at a situation where God's Word is being shared, sometimes we can be focused on the form, tangible things such as numbers, buildings, those kinds of things. But God is looking obviously at the heart, the real function of people's lives. And so we need to have those eyes too so that we see the real change and the things that God intends, and we should celebrate that even if the appearance is small and unimpressive.

? DISCUSSION POINTS

1. As you watch the tutorial video, note your observations about the speakers' level of understanding of the culture they live and work in. In that situation, what importance would you place on gaining these kinds of insights? How would you go about gaining cultural understanding and do you feel equipped to do that now?

2. When and how do you think a church should develop its 'forms' for; worship, music, meeting, teaching, baptism, discipleship, training, etc? How much should this development be guided by any cross-cultural church planters, or should it exclusively be shaped by the local body of believers? Please give your reasoning.

9.17 Reproducing this life

> ✓ **OBJECTIVES OF THIS TUTORIAL**
>
> This tutorial looks at the fifth question under the area of Life: 'Are they growing in their commitment to reproducing the life they have in Christ, are they equipped with the resources and skills to do so, and are they prioritizing opportunities where there is real need and hunger?'

> John 15:8: When you produce much fruit, you are my true disciples. This brings great glory to my Father.

That verse brings us to what we're wanting to focus on in this session. As we're talking about life, you may be thinking, "Okay what kind of life are we actually talking about?" When we go out and follow the Great Commission in making disciples and seeing people come to Christ, what are we looking for? And when bodies of believers come to know Him and follow Him, what is it that we're looking for? Are we just happy that they know Him? Or is there more to it? We see over and over again in Scripture that God really wants us to be believers who are bearing much fruit.

We'll be discussing discipleship in the next section. But here the focus is on fruit. We need to see the fruit and see where's there's real life, whether that be from an individual or from a group of believers in a church.

Last time

We looked at the fourth question from the WILD outline in the area of Life. We discussed how a group of believers learns to shape the form of what they do to serve whatever function they believe will lead to the fulfillment of God's purposes. In this tutorial we will discuss the fifth question in the WILD outline in the area of Life.

Are they growing in their commitment to reproducing the life they have in Christ, are they equipped with the resources and skills to do so, and are they prioritizing opportunities where there is real need and hunger?

Bill talks about how the elders from one of the churches faced challenges as they looked for more young men to bring into the teaching and outreach ministry:

> The elders brought up early the whole idea of how they train other people. They started realizing this job was huge, and they needed more help. And that

was just in the one church there. And so we talked to them about bringing young men or other men that were able to be teachers. They would be trained in the whole process. It was really hard for them because in one sense they're just learning themselves how to do this. And at that point to bring other men in and try to change them was really difficult. So we didn't push on that a whole lot. We were watching the elders grow. But over the last couple of years we've really seen them turn a corner in that once they'd been established and they realized what the Lord has been able to help them do. They're really excited about looking towards some of the young men and bringing other men on and training them.

Lots of questions have come from them in this last year really, such as, "Can we bring this guy on, let him teach a little?" Yes! You know, we're just always trying to encourage them to do that. I think, on the broader perspective of not just in the village itself but in the neighboring language groups, we've seen a huge desire because there's family in some of the other villages. They have a huge desire on their part to want to see the Gospel be taken over to the different churches or to the different villages. And that has resulted in other churches that have been born in other languages, not only in our language group but in the bordering language group. So we're watching them take what they know and want to transfer that to other people.

And it's not just about the identity of having a church. The drive has really been the hope. It's one of the things that just really drives the people where we're at, this whole thing of hope. What are we hoping for? What's going to happen to us when we die? Where are we going? And so when they start realizing that, they start getting this huge desire to want to see their family members understand this. And so there's been a huge drive for the church to branch out into the different places and see the Gospel taken over to the different areas.

Are they realizing that their willingness to associate with Jesus' death is directly linked to them having a part in His life being reproduced in others?

Are they seeing that, whatever other helpful relationships are involved, the primary accountability structure for equipping, caring for and guiding members in ministries should come from their local church?

Are they evaluating and aligning their efforts to share Christ's life (local or international) with the priorities, values and ministry strategies that the leadership team has clarified for the church as a whole?

Greg talks about the believers' desire to reach out to other communities, and to be better equipped to do so:

> The challenge for us wasn't teaching them to read and giving them a worldview perspective. They actually had a perspective that there was a world out there that didn't know Christ, especially in their own country. And so they've actually now begun to really look for opportunities and ways that they can reach into communities around them that they can reach out into, not just in their own villages where they are, but actually reach into other areas of the world.
>
> They're actually planning right now. They're going to even other countries and sending out some workers to other countries, and so part of their interest right now is in the area of training and the area of discipleship. How do they actually train guys up? How do they prepare people now to walk into other countries? How do they get them to enter into these areas? The heart that they have and the way that they understood church planting came from a perspective that they can become a part of the community, learn to grow in the community, learn to build relationships in that community.
>
> They've actually been wondering now about the process of cross-cultural communication. How do they actually learn that? How do they understand how to build and present that message clearly to the other places?

John describes how the church developed forms that were appropriate for the culture there as well as being profitable for God's work:

> Well, as far as forms within the church, their meetings were on Monday, Wednesday, and Friday. Then we cut it down to twice a week. And then we eventually moved it to Sunday. We were slow to do that because of the whole Sunday thing that was so fearful to them. But they didn't have a problem with that. As we taught the book of Acts, they started to see how the early church functioned. And so things like baptism were introduced, as they encountered it in the book of Acts. Communion, the Lord's supper...for that they went and they cut down bamboo and made little bamboo cups. And we just colored the water red. And so we made sure that we did things in a way that they could continue on. It wasn't dependent on us bringing in anything for them all. It had to be something that they could do and replicate in other

places as we anticipated churches would be planted in other places.

For Bible study times they would get together during the evening or sometimes during the day, depending on who they were and what they were involved in. And as more and more Scripture was translated, Bible teachers started to develop who would lead people and lead these Bible studies. But at the same time there was this awareness that there's still a lot of people from that language group who don't know Christ and who need to know Christ. And to reach some of those people was very, very difficult. So evangelism was always something that was in the forefront of their thinking. We had some young men who were very, very capable teachers. And they were usually guys who had been involved in the translation process or lesson development. That was tremendous grounding for them in learning God's Word and being able to share it with others.

In the last case study, John touched on the theme of the previous tutorial to do with form and function. But then he talked about how that then moved into the outreach of the church and the function of it. The church doesn't exist as an empty form or a religious tradition. The function, or the reason it exists is to be a place for the believers, for protection and for them to have this place of coming together to be fed God's Word and to worship. But it shouldn't end there, should it? That is what John is describing. They developed these forms to serve those functions of celebrating Christ's death together and to sing and to meet together. But then it flowed into the reaching out of the church. And we don't have the time to go into all the forms that might develop in the outreach of the church. It's just another part of the church functioning.

The question for this tutorial is, "Are they growing in their commitment to reproducing the life they have in Christ? Are they equipped with resources and skills to do so? Are they prioritizing opportunities where there is real need and hunger?" And that's what we want to see. That would be the real evidence of whether the life of Christ is now existing in a community. That is born of the conviction that the best representative of Christ here on this earth is the corporate body, the local group of believers together, not just as individuals, but as the whole. And together we grow to reach that level of maturity where we are reflecting Christ as a corporate body.

? DISCUSSION POINTS

1. In your view is Western-style seminary training ever something that would be appropriate for new leaders and teachers in a minority-group church planting situation? What would you see are some of the advantages and disadvantages?

2. A comment was made in the video directly linking a local church being genuinely indigenous in its form and function, and that church being able to reach out and reproduce itself throughout their people group and beyond. Please share any thoughts you have about this connection.

3. Research at least six mission agencies online. Note particularly whether they describe any strategies for church planting and for seeing churches grow on to maturity.

9.18 Disciples of the Master

✓ OBJECTIVES OF THIS TUTORIAL

This tutorial looks at the first question under the area of Discipleship: 'Are they seeing all other ties, loyalties, and commitments being increasingly defined by their primary relationship; disciples of their master, Jesus Christ?'

> Colossians 2:6: And now, just as you accepted Christ Jesus as your Lord, you must continue to follow him. Let your roots grow down into him, and let your lives be built on him. Then your faith will grow strong in the truth you were taught, and you will overflow with thankfulness.

This verse tells us who we're going to build our faith on, and it's Christ. We're thinking now about the subject of discipleship, and that's ultimately what is at the heart of the Great Commission. In the Greek, the idea here wasn't so much going; it was as we're going. As we're going, we need to be making disciples, not of ourselves, but of Christ.

As our roots grow down into Him and are built on Him, things will flow naturally out of that. Hopefully you see that discipleship includes theoretical truth, if you like, that's presented and we teach, but then it gives its real roots and its reality in everyday life. The verse above says that as you follow Him as His disciples, your faith will grow strong in the truth you were taught, and then you'll overflow with thankfulness.

Last time

We looked at the fifth and last question from the WILD outline in the area of Life. It focused on the area of growing in a commitment to reproduce the life that they have, and prioritizing ministry opportunities. In this tutorial we will discuss the first question in the WILD outline in the area of Discipleship.

Keep in mind that we're talking about allegiances here; our ultimate allegiance needs to be to Jesus Christ alone. In some countries, students put their hands over their chests and pledge allegiance to their countries' flag. But as you think about it, is our ultimate allegiance to the flag or what it represents? It's not God's intent for our ultimate allegiance to be to anything other than Christ Himself.

Discipleship is described and perceived in different ways, and specifically the issue of becoming a disciple and whether that means salvation comes after forsaking every other allegiance. What we see in Scripture is that Jesus' disciples did turn from whatever else they were following. There is a sense in which they put that aside. They left the nets and their families and followed Him. That's part of it. On the other hand, it's an ongoing process of discovering those things that are our allegiances. For unbelievers, they already have loyalties and allegiances. And so discipleship is also an ongoing process.

Are they seeing all other ties, loyalties and commitments being increasingly defined by their primary relationship; disciples of their Master, Jesus Christ?

Kelley talks about how identity as a disciple of Christ begins early on as people hear God's Word and continue to grow through suffering:

> Early on, through the Creation to Christ teaching and then up until Ephesians, I think that we have this visual of two bamboo holders up on two posts and so as you're going through Creation to Christ, you're constantly putting the two clans, Esau and Jacob, and they're making that identity. So, even early on, I feel like they realized that as believers they were disciples of Christ and that His road was going to be their road. As you're studying His life and all those things, they understand that that is going to be their life now, and so they're identifying with that. And then, as they grow, I think the most growth is done in the time of suffering. I think suffering is that gift that He gives us. He promises that we'll each suffer, if we even desire godliness. That's the time that we seek growth.

> I'll never forget—it was a couple months ago—there was some talk that had come up. In our village context, to have your name called to be accused of something is a tremendous sin, if it's not true. We had one of our believers that had her name called, and it was over something that she hadn't done. The unbelievers were accusing her of certain things and it was quite heavy for her. So I went over to visit with her and I just asked her, "Amelia, how are you doing with all this? How are you dealing with it?" She said, "Well, Joshua [her husband] and I just sat down and prayed. We just sat down and prayed about it because, from what we know about the Bible and the life of Christ, we are going to suffer just like He suffered."

> She had a passage in Matthew and a passage in Psalms. She's reading these through and it's like, "This is the road that I have for you." In her mind, it was

very clear. He suffered. We will suffer too. Our reward is not going to be in this world. It says that the world will hate us. It says these things so it's going to be true. Our rest is going to be in Heaven. It was just an encouragement to us to see. We didn't go over those passages with her. I don't even know how she found them, it had to be through her own study, but those were the things that the Lord was showing her and she understood that she was a disciple of Christ, that she would have to follow in those same footsteps.

Are they realizing that the relationship with Jesus is unique from all others in terms of its scope and rightful claims, and because it gives them access to His guidance in handling all other relationships correctly?

Are new believers being given help by other disciples as they face the challenges of reconfiguring their existing personal commitments and obligations in light of the relationship they've entered into with Jesus?

Are the individuals or teams in discipleship roles truly encouraging other believers in their commitments to Jesus as Master, or are they—perhaps unknowingly—fostering unhealthy individual and corporate allegiances?

John shares about seeing the believers begin to follow the model of discipleship that had been passed on to them:

> I think there was an emphasis on the fact that we're to grow in Christ. We start off as babes in Christ, but then as God's Word becomes more real to us and we understand more and more of it, we become stronger in our faith, in our dependence on God, in our love for Him, in our adoration of Him. That all impacts our lives and it impacts our relationships with other people, but in order to grow we need to connect with other believers who can help us in that journey. Initially, it was the church planters discipling, but then it was these guys who've been discipled discipling others. I think of an outreach with a young couple, and them taking another young couple with them and discipling them in church planting, that sort of thing happening.

Bill talks about the deepening discipleship relationship the church planting team had with the believers as they reached out, working with them as equals:

> It's funny because in that time where the new church starts becoming independent, a lot of workers start thinking about leaving them. Yet, that's

the very time that you can start working with them as equals. It's also in that time that you can start having discussions and talk about things that you've never been able to talk about before, just like you can with your teenage kids. It's the same way a teenage kid sometimes just walks away from their parents and is on their own, but yet I've seen a lot of teenagers have really good relationships with their parents during that time. It's during that time that they're open to talk about things that they've never talked about before. Right now, with the elders in the church, and they're basically in charge and I'm their helper, they see me more as an equal. I think it's this time period that I'm able to talk with them more about things that relate to the spiritual life. I can be vulnerable with them and they can be vulnerable with me. Whereas before they almost thought of us as never sinning. In fact, they even almost said as much; "Well, you never do that. We do this." Yet, now they're starting to see us in a much different light. It opens up a lot of discussions that we've never had before. I don't know how we would've talked about those things early on.

In the case studies in this tutorial, there's a strong sense of humility amongst the church planters. It's not a fake thing for church planters to be somehow portraying equality with the elders and wider body, but rather recognition that they are also disciples of Christ and also have great needs.

We began this tutorial with the question, "Are they seeing all the other ties, loyalties, and commitments being increasingly defined by their primary relationship; disciples of their Master, Jesus Christ?" We saw that this is for both the church planter and the wider church body; we are all disciples of Jesus Christ and we're growing and moving on this journey together.

❓ DISCUSSION POINTS

1. Spend some time reflecting on the verse that was shared in the tutorial (Colossians 2:6). Share any thoughts you have on how it relates to your own personal discipleship relationship with the Lord Jesus, particularly as you consider a future role in cross-cultural ministry.

2. What would you see are some of the implications when a church planter has a strong sense of their own national identity? Do you think patriotism can be an obstacle to modelling a primary loyalty to Jesus in a cross-cultural situation?

3. What kind of relationship are you eventually hoping to have with local believers where you live, specifically in terms of discipleship?

9.19 Real-life applications

 OBJECTIVES OF THIS TUTORIAL

This tutorial looks at the second question under the area of Discipleship: 'Are they being helped to apply the general truth from God's Word to their own specific real-life situations?'

1 Corinthians 13:2: If I had the gift of prophecy, and if I understood all of God's secret plans and possessed all knowledge, and if I had such faith that I could move mountains, but didn't love others, I would be nothing.

Last time

We looked at the first question from the WILD outline in the area of Discipleship. We talked about how all other ties, loyalties and commitments are increasingly defined by the primary relationship; disciples of their master, Jesus Christ. In this tutorial we will discuss the second question in the WILD outline in the area of Discipleship.

Are they being helped to apply the general truth from God's Word to their own specific real-life situations?

There's an obvious link between the verse above from first Corinthians and this question that we're asking. We're wanting to see people have truth and be disciples of Christ, not just digest knowledge. Love is not just the ability to stand in front of others and impart knowledge. In a religious setting, that could even be accepted as being okay and all that's needed. Real life, though, is reflective of Christ. We know that Christ didn't just speak words and impart knowledge and truth. He actually lived a life of serving and loving others and the way He cared for others and the way He spoke to their hearts met their needs. It was more than just words.

We saw the relationship Jesus had with His immediate disciples, the twelve. We saw so many times that He would speak to increasingly large crowds then spend time with the disciples talking about how to apply it in real life. His love for them is echoed in first Corinthians thirteen; it's the same love. Love is patient and kind. Love is not jealous or boastful or proud…love never gives up. It never gives up, never loses faith. It's always hopeful and it endures in every circumstance. If we're going to be good disciples, that's what we've got to be, haven't we? We've got to be hopeful of those who stumble and act like idiots sometimes. We all do. The Lord is like that with us, isn't He? He believes in us. He is hopeful, regardless of what we do so many times.

The disciples were often boasting and arguing, even up to the end. It says, "Love is not boastful" but they're boastful and wondering who will be the greatest in the kingdom of God. He's patient with them and He continues to love them to the end. He models discipleship for us.

As church planters, we'll see people who don't know Him yet and they'll be acting like people in darkness. Yet, as we get to know them and live in their community, we have to have that hope. Again, that love and hope comes only from Him. Picturing them as believers, as coworkers, as people who are going to be disciples of the Master and what their lives can become can help us keep trusting for that.

As they read, study, or hear God's Word being taught, do they see it as communication from a real Person who's always there and vitally interested in their daily lives, or is it more a religious activity they're participating in?

Dave talks about what practical discipleship looked like in the culture there where there the Spiritual was part of everyday life:

> Once they became saved, we continued with the regular public teaching meetings. We weren't teaching five and six days a week like we were initially. Still, we would have regular teaching meetings generally at least two days per week. They would come in from their gardens and everyone would be there. Along with the public teaching meetings, we wanted to continue to spend time with them in their daily lives as different things came up, as they faced various questions in life. We wanted to help them work through those and know how to apply God's Word to everyday life. Honestly, there are some ways that it's perhaps easier for them than it is for us in our culture because we tend to make more of a strict dichotomy between the spiritual elements of our lives and the everyday physical or just the common daily elements of our lives, such as work and family. There are a lot of people in our culture who have times where they're just really focused on their work or other aspects of just living in their home. Then they redirect their focus and now they're more specifically focused on God and their spiritual lives.
>
> The people we worked among historically never separated the spiritual realm from the physical. In some ways, it was almost more natural for them to just

keep the spiritual elements of Biblical truth intertwined with just the normal affairs of their daily lives. Sometimes, if someone in our culture is facing a particular question and we quickly spiritualize it, it can even feel a little bit awkward or forced. That's never the case with these people. It's just very natural to talk about God and about spiritual truths along with just normal everyday life because to them, they have never made any kind of distinction between the spiritual side of life and the physical side of life.

Is there a conscious effort being made to evaluate and, where possible, adjust the form in which Truth is taught to the gathered church so that it encourages discipleship in the body?

Palava explains that they prioritize equipping young people for the time when they have to go out into the world, to school, to find work, etc.

> Something very important to us is helping our children who have put their faith in Christ. Particularly, when they finish school and begin to be involved in the wider world. There are many challenges for them out there related to their understanding of God's Word. Our encouragement to them is based on God's Word that they have already heard in the church. We don't want to give advice that is founded in anything other than that. We want them to understand God's purposes for them. We want them to be able to make good choices about what things are profitable and what things are not because some of the things they learn out there are helpful, but other things are very destructive. We say to them, "Yes it is good for you to go and God is with you as you go. But the important thing is that you learn to evaluate everything based on what you have been taught from God's Word because that is the source of real understanding that you can count on." That is how we try to help our young people in their lives.

Greg describes how discipleship of younger believers is a priority for the church:

> As these guys have begun to reach out into their community and as they've begun to reach in and draw new life into the church, one of the aspects that they've wanted to do is to multiply as a body and to bring this understanding of God's Word and how to understand God's Word and how to describe it to themselves. Taking time to disciple and to mentor young believers in the Word of God, to invest in their lives, has been a big part of the church. Because of the ability and language that they have, they have extra-curricular materials that they can bring in to understand things as well. They can bring it out of books and study it.

> They're also learning just to take God's Word as it says and understand it, to read it, to teach from it, and to impart it into their lives.

Are there opportunities made for smaller groups (including one-on-one scenarios) to process, discuss and make relevant, practical applications from the teaching that is being given to the whole church?

Bill explains how the church planting team was conscious of strengthening family life as they taught and he describes the results of that:

> I think early on, when the church was born, one of the things that we stressed was the whole idea that God expects every man to be a teacher. That meant that every man needed to learn Scriptures so that he could teach his own family. We put the responsibility of teaching the family not just on the main church service, but as a whole for the community that they were each to meet as a family somehow. Whether that meant just husband, wife, kids, or clan, however that was going to look. It's interesting. About five or six years later if you look at the church, you see the ones that are growing and are strengthened are the ones that have continued to do that. A couple weeks ago I was actually in the village visiting. There are two elders that live side by side. Each evening they get together with their families and they read through some Scripture and just explain it to their children. That is one way that it's not just in the church service but it's in those ones that have taken on this idea of training their family in their life in general and they are the ones that are definitely growing and understanding the Scripture more.
>
> I sat and listened to them as they were in the evening training their children and teaching their family. Because it's more conversational, they were able to talk about things in a conversation. Whereas when there's teaching going on, you usually have one person teaching and then two or three hundred people sitting there listening to them teach. Whereas in the family, there's a lot of discussion going on and the two guys were sitting there asking their kids questions. Their kids were ranged from really small to older. They were just asking questions and talking through what they were studying, rather than just simply one guy just teaching it. That is definitely something that they are continuing to do. It's something I wish more than anything that more people in the church would do because definitely the result of that is just very clear. It's clear to everybody actually; the ones that take the time and effort to do that are just growing.

Kelley adds some more information about the elders meetings, teachers' meetings, ladies meetings, etc.

Early on we called them reading classes. They were like glorified Bible studies where we had the lessons. Like Bill said, we stressed the fact that every man needs to be able to teach because every man needs to be able to teach his family. It was open for all men. Early on there were quite a few people that came to that. That was a really good time to teach them how to read and to increase their literacy skills, to talk about the lesson, to know how to ask questions and give them some points of conversation that they could have with their families later. Over time what you saw is that it gets down to those faithful ones, right? It slowly diminished and then you have this faithful group of pretty much what is now our Bible teachers and our elders and our deacons. They meet on Thursdays, just kind of themselves. Then it's an open meeting as well. They meet and then it's in an open-air building. Others can come and they just plan out the week.

They plan out what issues they need to take care of, disputes in the village that they're accountable to give some input into. Anything that was coming up in the church or functions that they're going to get together and do. They plan all that out on Thursday. Then they talk about the lesson. They assign some things for Sunday and then they meet again on Sunday. The ladies are meeting once a week and going through a book of the Bible. They're going to redo the Creation to Christ teaching for their kids. They've seen that as a need.

We began this tutorial with the question, "Are they being helped to apply the general truth from God's Word to their own specific real-life situations?"

In each of the examples above we saw that discipleship takes intentionality. It takes a real commitment to being a discipler in order to see discipleship happen. As believers we need to be intentional. We need to have the conviction that this is what God would have us to do. We need to get to the place where it is a natural thing to bring others on into the work and to instill values of being part of the work of the church. We need to remind ourselves not to let that commitment go and to remember that it is a vitally important part of what we're doing. And we must remember that just because we have taught something doesn't necessarily mean that we are discipling.

REAL-LIFE APPLICATIONS

? DISCUSSION POINTS

1. As you watch the video, make note of any examples given of God's Word being applied to day-to-day life in the different contexts. In your own words describe how discipleship might have contributed to these positive outcomes in the churches.

9.20 Applying truth in the walk of faith

✓ OBJECTIVES OF THIS TUTORIAL

This tutorial introduces the third question in the area of Discipleship: 'Are they able to access regular, godly input and genuine friendships that intentionally help them along as they follow Jesus in the walk of faith?'

> John 17:17-19: Make them holy by your truth; teach them your word, which is truth. Just as you sent me into the world, I am sending them into the world. And I give myself as a holy sacrifice for them so they can be made holy by your truth.

These are the words of the Lord Jesus as He was speaking to the Father, of course, talking about the way that He'd been with His disciples. And it's such an amazing reflection of His heart, as He speaks to the Father about His relationship with those who God had given Him to be with.

Jesus is obviously thinking forward to His crucifixion here. It's interesting that we're called to be a living sacrifice, in the same way Jesus was a living sacrifice too. Even before He actually died on the cross, He was making Himself available to them. There were many times where He was tired and was ready to get away. But there were those who wanted to hear, and He would make Himself available to them.

There was a sense in which the disciples were like adolescents at times. In some ways they were so petty. But Jesus was patient and willing to be accessible and just to be with them. For those of us who have a role in church planting, it's crucial to see this time with unbelievers and new believers as a precious opportunity to perhaps equip them for something they'll face once we're gone.

Last time
We looked at the second question from the WILD outline in the area of Discipleship. It asked if people are being encouraged to apply truth to their own real-life situations. In this tutorial we will discuss the third question in the WILD outline in the area of Discipleship.

Are they able to access regular, godly input and genuine friendships that intentionally help them along as they follow Jesus in the walk of faith?

There are a few words there, perhaps, that we could really focus on that will help us to consider what's involved. Having genuine friendships conveys intentionality. When you start putting all those words together the sum total actually involves a lot of sacrifice. It means a lot of giving up what we see as our own rights. It means giving up "me time", which is prevalent in Western society. It means not looking out for number one all the time.

The Lord can use situations where we have little time to ourselves to teach us to be accessible, to be available to give godly input. If our hearts aren't ready for that and we're just thinking about ourselves and how annoying the interruption is then we won't be ready to give that godly input. Instead we'll see it as a hindrance. And yet, discipleship requires that we be willing to let go at any time and be available to those who have needs.

For those of us who are involved in church planting, there will be deadlines or office work that really needs to be done. There'll be lessons to prepare and a team to lead. Your family will need you also and that's important too. There will be all these competing things. It's so important to trust the Lord that He'll bring the balance in those relationships so that we will be accessible and available to these folks who are the reason we're there.

It probably means that there's no longer just the idea of working nine to five or having a set time that we're available. If we have that mentality, we'll miss out on so many opportunities that are actually the whole reason that we're there in the first place.

It may mean maybe changing our schedules. For those of us who like to keep schedules and specific times for doing things this will be especially difficult. We still have to do our work, but when people need us, then we'll have to try to be there for them and say to the Master, "Okay, we know that You're available and so we need to be as well."

Is the subject of relational discipleship being taught and discussed in a way that communicates its true value and necessity in the life of individuals and the group?

Are there those who, although very conscious of their own needs, are actively pursuing friendships with other believers with the purpose of encouraging them to follow Him as disciples?

Greg describes how discipleship in Siberia often happened as people lived life and spent time together:

> As the church began to grow, one of the main key components that we saw in Scripture was this idea of mentoring and discipling and investing into lives and teaching others. So we began partnering with different men and women in the group. Our wives were meeting with the ladies, my teammate David also partnered and we were discipling and mentoring the men and women of the community. It looked different maybe than how we perceived it.
>
> So much of what we see in the West now is a perception that you do it in a coffee shop for an hour a day or whatever it is and you do that once a week. It was very different in the sense of it was life with life, we lived life together. We would be very much involved with each other's lives, where they worked, where I worked with students. You were walking life with them, along with them, and teaching them how a godly man should live. We went through a whole group of guys. For most of the men of the community, alcoholism is a problem by the time you're sixteen years old. Your destiny is that you'll be dead by the time you're forty-five. So for these guys to actually watch life being lived out, for older men, "How do they live, how do you treat your wives, how do you treat your husbands, how do you actually treat your children, what should you do at work, how should you respond to parents who don't like how you are as a believer and how should you be a father or mother?"
>
> Dealing with all those real-life issues was done in many different ways. We did things where we would take guys on these camping trips, long hikes all the way across Siberia, across the lakes, over the mountains. We did a variety of things where you could get away with men and teach men what men were like and teach how God wanted us to be as believers. And the same with the women, they would get together and disciple each other and invest in each other's lives and keeping that going. One of the challenges in that is to maintain that intensity and that's where the church is struggling at these times. Where they're walking through it and actually continuing that all the way along where people's lives are being invested in each other. And it's something that, as churches grow, seems to drift or dwindle a little bit and one of the challenges they're facing right now is figuring out how that can proceed in the future.

Are there opportunities for discipleship relationships to develop into genuine partnerships of equality and trust in the context of service?

Matt describes the challenges for discipleship in the context where they work:

> We need to help. We need to walk alongside of them and feel what they feel and help them discover how they can love their family and truly not be concerned about reputation. It's easy enough for this ex-pat to say; I'm from another place and my reputation is not at stake with these people. I believe we need to spend more time with them and ask the harder questions about how to continue to be a part of their community, continue to be a part of their family.
>
> In real practical terms, I think we need to sit down and talk about whether or not they should participate in activities that are not religiously driven but are socially driven but where the stigma of drunkenness and alcoholism and all of that is still part of the scene and help them ask, "What would a believer do in that? Would he separate himself from that? Would he not engage in the sin of that but come alongside and participate as a member of the community in that?" And I think that's where our discipleship needs to go instead of being on the outside and watching them suffer through that, coming alongside and really walking with them in that and really asking them to engage in God's Word together with us. Really get alongside and ask them to engage with God's Word with us to determine what it would look like for them to live in that society and be a light to their people.

So in other words, we really don't have the answers, I don't believe. I think what we are seeing is that we need to join them and really help them come to the Word of God and really wrestle well with what it means to be a Christian in their society as an insider.

We started this tutorial with the question, "Are they able to access regular Godly input and genuine friendships that intentionally help them along as they follow Jesus in the walk of faith?" We didn't focus too much on the area of intentionality, we'll get to that in subsequent tutorials, but hopefully what's come across is this idea of really being available and really prioritizing genuine friendships so that the teaching of God's Word is applied in real life circumstances. And that happens through everyday discipleship.

TUTORIAL 9.20

➡ ACTIVITIES

1. Do some online research and see how much different mission organizations focus on discipleship and how they describe it. Summarize your findings and share any thoughts you have.

2. In a short paragraph describe 'Disciple Making Movements'. Please share your thoughts on what you discover, if possible using the broader WILD categories.

9.21 Equipped for Service 1

OBJECTIVES OF THIS TUTORIAL

This tutorial introduces the fourth question in the area of Discipleship: 'Are they encouraged to function in the areas in which God has gifted and given the abilities so they can develop in their service to Him and His body?'

> Romans 12:4: Just as our bodies have many parts and each part has a special function, so it is with Christ's body. We are many parts of one body, and we all belong to each other.

Paul gives this statement after his exhortation to be a living sacrifice, and now he applies that specifically to the service of the body. He makes the point that the body has different functions. Good discipleship recognizes the different functions. It's not a cookie cutter formula, but it recognizes and encourages different functions in the body.

We need to be looking for opportunities for those gifts to be used. By default, we might be quick to recognize a certain type of gift, possibly the gifts that are similar to ours may be the easiest to spot. It's important to learn about the different types of gifts that God has given and to see those being used. That requires, though, that we understand what they are and how they can best fit into the body. There's this idea of individuals with gifts all being encouraged to serve the body. There's a sense of mutual ownership of those gifts.

Last time

We looked at the third question from the WILD outline in the area of Discipleship. We discussed the importance of people having access to regular, Godly input and intentional friendships that help them along as they follow Jesus in the walk of faith. In this tutorial we will discuss the fourth question in the WILD outline in the area of Discipleship.

Are they being encouraged to function in the areas in which God has gifted and given them abilities so they can develop in their service to Him and His Body?

We want to see people functioning in line with the gifts that God has given them. We want to avoid forcing square pegs into round holes, to be sensitive to the way that God has made each individual. Often gifts don't reveal themselves clearly until people start to serve, then we can start encouraging them to use their gifts and help them to even recognize it themselves, as well as have others recognize it and support them in it. That's a really important part of discipleship.

That comes back to what we said previously, which is just how important it is for us to know the people that we're working with, to have those relationships with them. One thing that comes to mind here too is how it ties back into the narrative flow right from the beginning, starting with God's intention for His image bearer, Adam. There we see the origins of discipleship where He gives them a task. They're to represent Him on the earth and to flourish and to spread out and to be His representatives here. He teaches them and guides them in that. We see that pattern all throughout the Old Testament with individuals in different times who were raised up and who had God given functions or roles. God didn't just give those jobs but He also walked alongside people in that and always in light of the purpose He had for them. Then in the flow of history, Jesus chose these men, His disciples, and appointed them, gave them His word to pass on, put churches into place, and then that continues on to the next generation of the Church.

So, we see that progression coming down into the Church; God's intention and that cycle of passing it on from one to the other. Even as churches were coming to maturity in Acts, we see that Paul told Timothy and Titus to have elders recognized in each of the locations, men who were set aside to help lead these groups, not just a directionless discipleship but they actually move with purpose and want to see certain things accomplished. That comes back to the different gifts that God has given the body. In Ephesians 4:11-12 it says, "He gave the apostles, the prophets, the evangelists, the shepherds and teachers, to equip the saints for the work of ministry, for building up the body of Christ." So we see even today there are people that God has set aside for the growth of the church and they have particular gifts and so we need to recognize those and actually encourage them to use them.

One of the things that is often a hindrance to the process of people using their gifts is our lack of recognition of them or when we don't have a means for them to use them. That can happen when we have the view of the "professional". in some cultural settings, that's the way it is, but when we come into these settings we shouldn't bring into them, by default, our view of the clergy or insist on seminary training before people can begin to function in leadership. God has raised those people up from within local bodies, and without getting into saying that something is wrong or right, certainly this is the pattern we see in Scripture, like the obvious passage in 2 Timothy 2:1-2 where Paul says, "Timothy, my dear son, be strong through the grace that God gives you in Christ Jesus, and what you have heard from me in the presence of many witnesses entrust to faithful men who will be able to teach others also."

We should be passing the truth on to people who are faithful and be looking for them and believing that God will raise them up from within local fellowships that are planted in these different places. It's incredibly important for us to have that as an end goal then, and not something short of that because if it's something shorter, then they're going to reach a certain place but after that they're going to look around and there will be no more opportunity. They won't be actually able to use the gifts that God has given them for the growth of the whole body and so it will remain stunted in its growth.

We can develop ways to promote growth, such as structures and systems, which aren't necessarily at odds with the friendship-based discipleship we're talking about. Churches need to know how to bring on those who are going to be the leaders and function in their areas of gifting. When the initial church planters are no longer there, they need to know how to bring on the next generation and how to see elders raised up and teachers equipped within the local body. It should continue past the first generation. That's the plan, that's what the narrative is all about really, isn't it?

Are they being discipled into areas of service or are they being held back by personal, systemic or cultural barriers?

Dave describes the cultural leadership structure that existed before the church was planted and how that affected the leadership that developed in the church:

> The patriarch of each clan was a leader and when it came to a village or even multiple villages coming together, these clan heads would get together. They were like the elders and they would come together and make decisions. If there was some kind of court case that needed to be handled, they're the ones that handled it. If there were serious decisions to be made, they are the ones who made the decisions for the entire village or even for the entire tribal group. Eventually, of course, we started teaching them about the qualifications for Biblical leadership within the church. These qualifications of course, were very, very different from the qualifications for being a tribal leader.

> The qualifications for being a tribal leader, well, first of all, it was an inherited position. It would be the oldest son among brothers within a clan. Then there were certain things that were expected of these leaders to where some of

them would rise above others, perhaps because of their ability and oratory, or their hard work and productiveness in gardens, and also owning many pigs. There were things like that that would help raise the status of some of these village elders above others. Of course, we taught them Biblical principles of what a Biblical leader within the church is supposed to be.

It was exciting to see that even some of these older men who didn't really qualify Biblically were able to fit into the structure of the church and see some of the younger men take the leadership roles in the church. Some of the older ones had disqualified themselves by marrying multiple wives or in other ways they just were not qualified to be church leaders and yet the churches have moved forward in this and it's been very encouraging to see the church as a whole understand what Biblical leadership is all about and recognize those leaders and give them the respect, that ear that they truly should give them and realizing that this really is God's way. That God's standards for leadership in the church need to be our standards.

John explains how evangelism was always in the forefront of the thinking of church leaders and how that motivated them to disciple more young men as Bible teachers:

As for Bible study times, they would get together during the evening or sometimes during the day, depending on who they were and what they were involved in. As more and more Scripture was translated, Bible teachers started to develop who would lead people and lead these Bible studies. At the same time, there was this awareness that there's still a lot of people from that language group who don't know Christ and who need to know Christ and to reach some of those people was very, very difficult. So, evangelism was always something that was in the forefront of their thinking. We had some young men who were very, very capable teachers. They were usually guys who had been involved in the translation process or lesson development, and that was tremendous grounding for them in learning God's Word and being able to share it with others.

So, the way that all happened was usually this: one of us would teach the lesson to these guys who would then be responsible to teach it to the church. Out of that group came those who went and planted churches.

John describes how leadership developed in the church and some of the challenges in that process:

There were a number of guys who helped with translation. Those guys were probably in the forefront of being developed as church leaders, although we would have meetings during the day for the men and anyone could come to those meetings. Those groups had this specific goal of raising up leaders, of teaching areas of truth that would really develop men who had a heart for the people, to shepherd the people. I can remember like groups of fifteen or sixteen men gathering together during the day to be taught. Not all of those guys ended up in leadership, but a number of them did. I think that's taken a long process and it's been interrupted because one of my team members, Keith, was just at the point where he was wanting to really concentrate on leadership development when the fighting broke out. The whole thing was disrupted and he was never able to really get into that as seriously as he'd hoped to be able to.

I'm sure that's a disappointment with the work. Had that not been the case we would have hoped that we'd had stronger leadership. That has been an area for prayer really that the men will accept responsibility, and there are a number who do. Some of them have been through some pretty discouraging times, some really hard times. Some of them, because of their families, have felt disqualified and it's nothing that they have actually done, but something that their families, their kids maybe have done. They've felt, "How can I lead the church if I can't lead my own family?" I know with one couple who were on outreach, their lives were threatened a number of times and eventually they came home. That was a real discouragement to them. So, there have been these discouraging times. There's been some real challenges for the church there.

Are opportunities being created for the expression of spiritual gifts and is there scope for people to explore appropriate ways to use their experience and skills?

Is there a paternalism that stifles the growth of younger, newer and less mature believers OR is there a vision for discipleship that actively works to bring them to places of equality and hands authority over in a timely way?

Greg explains how the leadership roles in the church encourage and facilitate discipleship taking place:

> One of the aspects, or functions, of the churches that we are talking about here is that they have roles of elders and we've appointed elders in these roles. These are guys that the Body of Christ identifies as leaders of the

church and these are the ones that take responsibility as far as the spiritual life, the teaching, the involvement with families, and investing in the spiritual levels of it.

There are also different roles in the church that exist, in the sense of deacon roles, where these guys are functioning and existing. When the original guys were brought in, we did appoint them, but these were men and women that had been discipled and mentored and trained over a number of years. They were actually functioning as elders before we ever appointed them as elders. They were already doing it. That's been the philosophy right along as the church has been adding new life on and new elders into the churches. These guys get brought on and these are usually men or women that are actually already functioning in those spiritual roles where they're discipling and are also mentoring other families and other individuals in those churches.

We started this tutorial with the question, "Are they being encouraged to function in the areas in which God has gifted and given them abilities so they can develop in their service to Him and His Body?" This question helps us evaluate where we're at and what to look for so that we can truly help one another. Our goal as church planters is to see people being encouraged to function in areas in which God has gifted them. We are hoping for the different individuals in the church body, along with their own gifts, to be given a place where they can actually function and be encouraged as they do so.

❓ DISCUSSION POINTS

1. A woman in the video described her life working alongside her husband in various roles in the church. For a couple seeking to disciple cross-culturally, how important do you think it is for both husband and wife to be involved in all aspects of the work? If you are married, have you talked about this together and how do you see it working?

2. Research how 'paternalism' is portrayed in the history of missions.

3. In your own words give a defence for this statement, "Paternalism obstructs discipleship."

9.22 Equipped for service 2

> ✓ **OBJECTIVES OF THIS TUTORIAL**
>
> This tutorial introduces the fifth question in the area of Discipleship: 'Do they have access to defined pathways that offer Bible-based resources, practical instruction and relational discipleship to adequately equip them to serve the church locally and globally?'

> Ephesians 2:10: For we are God's masterpiece. He has created us anew in Christ Jesus, so we can do the good things he planned for us long ago.

That is an encouraging verse for us to consider for our lives individually and also for those that we have the opportunity to rub shoulders with and pour our lives into, that they also are God's masterpieces and He has plans for them.

God planned good things for us long ago and that's the thing, isn't it? When our vision fails to see what can happen, we can lean on His vision, but at the same time, we're called to hope for these things and to have good strategies and to be intentional. There are situations where God does amazing things with people who the world considers of no significance and people who are, in the sense of the world, often poorly educated and marginalized people, the weak and the foolish.

In the case studies, it's exciting to share some of these things that God has done with those who are being prepared, with those of you who are being prepared for God's work. We are praying and trusting that this would be a help and an inspiration perhaps to those of you who are planning to go out to share God's Word and see a church planted in some unreached area. It's kind of cool to see that these are things that God has planned from so long ago, an eternity to play out, and it's wonderful to see this, His masterpiece.

Last time

We looked at the fourth question from the WILD outline in the area of Discipleship, which dealt with the area of people being able to exercise the gifts that God has given them so that they can develop in their service to Him and His body. In this tutorial we will discuss the fifth and last question in the WILD outline in the area of Discipleship.

Do they have access to defined pathways that offer Bible-based resources, practical instruction and relational discipleship to adequately equip them to serve the church locally and globally?

Practical instruction and relational discipleship are kind of the more tangible things that are reproducible. Do they have a good model, something that they can actually tangibly take and pass on? Do they have good material in their own hands? We have so much available when we're wanting to go and to speak or to share, there are just unlimited resources, certainly in English. Part of our role is to provide those kinds of resources for the church. If they are to one day go beyond the borders of their village or their local valley or their town, wherever it might be, to further afield, but if they're to do that, then they need to be equipped. For us to dream a little of them partnering with other churches, other efforts in their own country, and with folks like ourselves from other countries, and for those partnerships to take place all around the world, it will take intentionality. It means actually equipping folk to be able to do that properly as they move out.

Matt talks about how their dream for the church there fuels their day to day strategy among the believers in spite of the great challenges in that context:

> Our dream, our passion has been that God would build His Church there, that Christ would build His Church that would be a light to a dark society. As we think of the small group of believers that we have been able to be a part of seeing come to Christ, our dream is to build them up so that they would be a viable vibrant witness to their people. And so our focus is really right now on the believers and a few of the opportunities we have with unbelievers to really build into their hearts and lives a love for Christ that would compel them out and that they would somehow figure out how to communicate this love for Christ to their family and to their friends and to their neighbors. Because of the dynamics of the cartels and the drug scene there, we are very limited where we can go and who we can interact with. Even that component pushes us more into viewing our role as supporting and assisting that small band of believers to see the Gospel penetrate and the church to grow beyond where we're at right now.
>
> Probably in my heart, I've moved from the philosophy or the mentality that I could actually reach them to realizing that God has us there as being members of the body that's going to reach others and they are the body.
>
> We view ourselves as assisting the believers there in any way we can through

teaching, discipleship, and developing more curriculum. One of our biggest projects right now is to bring the written curriculum into an audio form so that we can get more people listening to the Word, listening to the teaching. Those are just different ways we want to assist them and we're doing all of that inside of the context of a Spanish-Mexican church.

We're doing all of that inside of the context of a Spanish-Mexican church and discipling that church to realize that the Great Commission of reaching the world is for them and we're just there to assist them. It's multi-faceted. It's very complex, but very exciting to live in that place and see Christ start to get the hearts of His children in that community for these people.

Is there a sense of responsibility taken in the church to be informed about current trends, needs and opportunities so that members can be given valid input as they move towards new opportunities for service?

Are the ministry values, priorities and objectives of the church shared regularly with the whole body, in smaller contexts, and in discipleship relationships?

Does the church have a vital interest and sense of responsibility in seeing all members properly equipped to be effective disciple-makers, OR do they draw a false dichotomy between "full-time, professional, specialists ministries" and other "normal walks of life"?

Bill talks about how important it is to have an overall plan for training teachers, developing leaders, and seeing them become equipped and personally responsible for their roles:

> Yeah, I think one of the key things is to have a strategy to actually get yourself there. People don't just naturally come to an understanding of something unless there's a plan to actually move them from not understanding it to understanding. I think early on, we saw people or teachers develop, we started out helping them understand how to present things. Then once they got good at presenting things, then we worked with them on how to actually add illustrations in and then, add application in.
>
> Over a period of time, as they grew in their ability to present information and then to teach it, it started coming more from the heart. The last stage

was actually leaving out a lot of the teachers' helps in the lessons and forcing them to actually think through why they were saying what they were saying. It was through that reflection, I believe, as they were teaching the Word of God and reflecting and as the Holy Spirit was giving them insights, that they started seeing all the connections between the different things that they had learned and studied.

Again, I just think it's important that you have a planned strategy to get there, not just assume that they're going to come to that point, but actually help develop them to get to that point.

Bill shares their encouragement in seeing the elders prioritize discipleship for God's purposes in reaching out to others:

The elders brought up early on the whole idea of how to train other people. They started realizing that this job was huge and they needed more help in just the one church there. We talked to them about bringing young men or other men that were able to be teachers and able to be trained and do the whole process. It was really hard for them because in one sense, they're just learning themselves how to do this and so to at that point to bring other men in and try train them was really difficult.

We didn't push on that a whole lot because again, we were just hoping, we were watching the elders grow, but over the last couple of years, we've really seen them turn the corner in that. Once they've been established and they realized what the Lord has been able to help them do, they're really excited about looking toward some of the young men and bringing other men on and training them. Lots of questions have come from them in this last year really of, "Can we bring this guy on, let him teach a little?" Yes! We're just always trying to encourage them in doing that.

I think on the broader perspective of not just in the village itself, but in the neighboring language groups…we've seen a huge desire because there's family in some of other villages. On their part there is a huge desire to want to see the Gospel be taken over to the different churches or to the different villages and that has resulted in other churches that have been born in the other language, not only in our language group, but in the bordering language group. We are watching them take what they know and want to transfer that to other people. And it's not just about the identity of having a church.

The drive to it has really been hope, because that's one of the things that just really drives the people where we're at. What are we hoping for? What's going to happen to us when we die? Where are we going? When they started realizing answers to that, they started getting this huge desire to see their family members understand this and so it's been a huge drive for the church to branch out to different places and see the Gospel taken over to the different areas.

John describes the challenging situation in the church today, but the comfort in knowing they have the Lord and His Word:

> The amazing and the wonderful thing is that they do have almost the New Testament finished and many, many portions of the Bible so they have God's Word. They've been well grounded in God's Word and have that tremendous foundation upon which there's a real confidence that they know God, that they have a relationship with Him. Everything's there to be able to bring these sparks back to life. The area that was all jungle when we moved in there has now become quite a center and I think the government's moving in there, the lumber companies have moved in and so the whole base Is becoming quite a commercial center. This is introducing challenges that they've never had before. I am really praying for them that they'll come through that well.

John's comments are sobering because in this world there are many challenges and we have an enemy who is trying to destroy the Church. As we give our lives for others and make disciples, we realize, as was mentioned earlier, that there are those who do fall away, ones who have so much potential and yet they waste it. It's a very sad thing. Churches themselves have many challenges that face them and a lot of them are minorities. As minorities, they themselves have issues with others who are coming in and maybe have more education and can take advantage of them.

As master builders, what God intends for us is to be ones who would foster an understanding of the challenges that are coming and so leave others prepared. It's true that we can't anticipate all the challenges that are going to come at them. Our responsibility is to give them God's Word and teach them, give them the whole counsel of God, and there's a lot there. That's not leaving them with little. That's leaving them with all they need.

As it says in 2 Peter 1:3, "His divine power is granted to us, all things that pertain to life and godliness through the knowledge of Him who called us to His own glory and excellence." We see that when we give them God's Word, they have all they need, regardless of the challenges and the difficult context.

EQUIPPED FOR SERVICE 2

> ➡ **ACTIVITIES**
>
> **1.** In about half a page, share your thoughts about anything that has particularly impacted you as you have gone through this module. Note any specific areas where your thinking has changed, or where you are still considering the implications of something you heard.

ACCESSTRUTH

Training Resources for Making Truth *Accessible*.

RESOURCES FOR

- Discipleship
- Evangelism
- Church Planting
- Language Learning
- Bible Translation
- Cross-cultural work

Equipping God's people to be more effective as they serve in cross-cultural contexts, either locally or globally.

accesstruth.com

www.ingramcontent.com/pod-product-compliance
Lightning Source LLC
Chambersburg PA
CBHW061812290426
44110CB00026B/2853